CONC

CONCILIUM
ADVISORY COMMITTEE

CONCILIUM 2021/4

Amazonia: Gift and Tasks

Edited by

Geraldo L. De Mori, Michelle Becka
and John Baptist Antony

Published in 2021 by SCM Press, 3rd Floor, Invicta House, 108–114 Golden Lane,
London EC1Y 0TG.

SCM Press is an imprint of Hymns Ancient & Modern Ltd (a registered charity)
13A Hellesdon Park Road, Norwich NR6 5DR, UK

www.concilium.in

ISBN 978-0-334-03160-4

Printed in the UK by
Page Bros, Norwich

Concilium is published in March, June, August, October, December

Contents

Part Three: Reflection on the Issue

Part Four: Response to the Issue

Theological Forum

Editorial
Amazonia: Gift and Tasks

Not only since the Amazon Synod, Amazonia has become a symbol. This region, apart from all centers, is nevertheless the center of attention, because here worldwide questions and problems show up and condense in a special way: ecological problems that affect everyone are more visible here than elsewhere. The close interweaving of ecological and social issues is also particularly evident: the threat to the ecosystem directly endangers the survival of people, especially the indigenous peoples. The vulnerability of the entire ecosystem and its inhabitants is high. It is exacerbated by massive interventions by (multinational) companies that ignore and violate human rights and rights of nature. The local consequences of global consumption practices and economics are enormous. Some scientists believe that the variant of the new coronavirus that appeared in Manaus is an indication of other possible consequences of the destruction of this biome. The categories local and global intertwine and blur.

The problems bring with them numerous challenges for theology, for the Church and for pastoral ministry. The Amazon Synod has been deeply involved in these issues. And here too, it became clear that manifestations may be specific - but similar challenges arise in pastoral work worldwide. It is therefore also necessary to examine which impulses can come from the pastoral experiences in the Amazon region for others - or also whether pioneering pastoral projects take place elsewhere that can be seriously challenged by the problems of the time and credibly go new ways.

However, the ecclesial and theological challenges are not limited to pastoral work alone. The amazon region is a theological place: unity can be experienced in diversity; if theology is consistently pursued from here, it changes theology - to do this is still more desideratum than reality (not only in the Amazonia). In the context of the Synod, it was said that

Amazon is Good Friday and Easter: suffering and joy lie close together. Suffering, because humans and environment are existentially threatened. Joy, because faith and *joie de vivre* can be experienced and solidarity plays an important role.

It is exciting that the network concept is gaining importance. In the region, Pan-Amazonian Ecclesial Network (REPAM) is improving awareness of the local people's concerns and is coordinating the cooperation of various bodies. In a similar way, the Ecclesial Network for the Congo River Basin (REBAC) has started its work. Both networks are also interconnected. In this way, new relations between Latin America and Africa emerge - beyond economic and dependency structures. Rather, they are relations of solidarity - a solidarity network has emerged. The Amazon region therefore also stands for hope and departure. This is also significant in other respects, for it can be interpreted as an example of decolonization. The Amazon region used to be (and still is) a space par excellence for exotic fantasies: indigenous peoples considered as savages and "quite different", a place of longing for gold prospectors and other adventurers... The inhabitants of the region, who have been altered and objectified in these discourses, today appear in the struggle for their rights as actors - this important change, too, is theologically significant and must be taken seriously.

The issue is divided into four parts. In the first one, the significance of the Amazon region and similar regions is analyzed; in particular, the ecological significance is central and is discussed in an interdisciplinary manner. **Carlos Nobre** (climatologist), **Ismael Nobre** (biologist) and **Maritta Koch-Weser** (anthropologist) present Amazonia 4.0, a project that seeks to offer to traditional communities living in the Amazon access to innovative technologies that generate income, at the same time, keep the forest standing. The Amazonia 4.0 project has two components: Creative Lab of the Amazon (CLA) to serve as an empowerment tool for communities aiming to add value in the cupuaçu-cacao chain and the Rainforest Business School (RBS) to structure a new field of business knowledge for a new generation of experts. The following text, by **Nicole Bernex**, proposes a study on the anthropic impacts of deforestation, especially in the equatorial regions of Africa and Asia, showing the importance of these biomes for the people who live there and how their destruction leads to increased poverty. The article recognizes the social and economic character of the ecological crisis, and shows that its Eco-ethical essence allows us to propose strategies that increase the resilience of ecosystems and the populations that depend on them. The contribution of **Gerhard Kruip** opens a social-ethical perspective on the issue of extractivism in Latin America. His thesis is that, in view of the urgency of the problem, it is not possible to wait until capitalism has been overcome before finding solutions. Rather, with the appropriate political will, targeted measures for a more socially just and sustainable policy of resource exploitation are already possible now.

The second part identifies and discusses the ethical and political challenges together with social impacts that are associated with this. **Léocadie Lushombo** shows how projects designed to mitigate climate change in Kongo simultaneously lead to ethical conflicts when they are designed to be too technology- and market-based. In particular, they jeopardize peacebuilding processes. The paper concludes that participation of local communities and relationships of trust in the management of the tropical forests are a crucial means of sustainable conservation and are a peacebuilding tool. **Cedric Prakash** starts his article referring to the film *The Mission* as an apt background to the post-synodal Apostolic Exhortation *Querida Amazonia* and discusses on the need and importance of addressing and acting on the wrongs inflicted on the people of God and on our common home. The author illustrates with examples the fact that human rights violation on the indigenous peoples, the poor and the other vulnerable groups and on earth happen all over the world, particularly in the Southern Hemisphere. Giving example from tribbles of India, he argues that the indigenous peoples are the most affected. Secondly, quoting Pope Francis heavily, he takes pain to convince that the ecological crisis is also about human rights. The article ends proposing some ways to go forward. **Birgit Weiler**'s contribution deals with the consequences of neo-extractivism and neo-colonialism in the Amazon and determines the potential of self-determined action of indigenous people through their organization in umbrella organizations and networks. Networks are reflected theologically as an expression of global solidarity in view of the extreme endangerment of Amazonia and its consequences, especially for the original peoples.

The third part of the issue reflects relevant theological questions from the systematic and the biblical theologies. **Fernando Roca Alcázar** argues that in the encounter between Catholic theology and the religious beliefs of the Amazonian peoples, nature plays an important role. The author believes that Moltmann's pneumatological theology of creation can help deepen inter-religious dialogue in the case of a specific Amazonian people: the Awajún-Wampis. Then follows the paper of **Cristino Robles** - Pope Francis challenges everyone to establish networks of solidarity to advance human dignity and the environment, respecting diversity. He considers the Amazon region as a theological locus. In connection with this, we know that Genesis 1:28 and its dominant interpretation has been for a long time used to justify human beings' abuse of the natural world. His paper, through a reader-oriented intertextuality, with "light" and "darkness" as keywords, offers an alternative way of reading Genesis 1:1–2:3 with Job 29:1-25. This reading highlights differentiation as God's gift to creation and solidarity as a human task. For **Victor Codina**, the Amazon synod caused a series of tensions in society and in the church. Ecclesial tensions are part of the polarity that runs through history between unity and diversity, between centralism and dispersion, between the universal Catholic Church and the local churches. According to the author, the overcoming of such theological and pastoral tensions can be enlightened from an ecclesial synodality and an updating of pneumatology.

The last part concludes with the presentation of pastoral projects and grassroot movements - from Amazonia and from Congo. **Mauricio López** affirms that the Amazonian synod has its origin in the territorial pastoral praxis that had its greatest development in the Pan-Amazonian Ecclesial Network (REPAM). This network, the author recalls, is the result of the incarnated experience of church members in this territory, who, with lights and shadows, have helped to delineate inculturated and intercultural pastoral perspectives, giving rise to an Amazonian face for the church. The synod, in connection with *Laudato si'*, opens new paths to respond to the most urgent challenges of the Amazonian territory, and as a paradigm for a reflection on the pastoral care of the whole church. **Rigobert Minani Bihuso**'s article describes the contribution of the Church Network of the Congo Basin (REBAC) to the social and environmental pastoral care of the Church in Africa. The author shows the meeting points between this network and the Pan-Amazonian Ecclesial Network (REPAM), showing how *Laudato si'*, the meeting of the African church and the Latin American church, have inspired ecological pastoral ministry in Africa. The article points out the priorities of this pastoral care as it emerges from the cartography of pastoral and socio-environmental challenges of the Congo basin. The article aims to spread and root this pastoral care of integral ecology, which articulates in-depth evangelization and environmental, economic and social engagement.

In the Theological Forum, two authors analyse the Instruction "The pastoral conversion of the Parish community in the service of the evangelizing mission of the Church", published by the Congregation for the Clergy, of 29.06.2020: **Martin Rehak** from a canonistic perspective, and **Caronila Bacher** from a pastoral and theological perspective.

The Final Document of the Synod of Amazonia was entitled "Amazonia: New Paths for the Church and for Integral Ecology". The different texts that make up this issue of Concilium invite us to discover the "newness", to which the synod invites us, as a gift and a task. In fact, the Pan-Amazon as well as the Congo basin and the tropical area of South Asia concentrate the greatest biodiversity of the planet, constituting a gift of the Creator to the world. However, with the gift also comes responsibility, the task of care. Hopefully, the reflections proposed here can contribute to awaken the churches and the theology, to the discovery of the importance of these biomes for life and the need to defend them for the future of the planet.

Geraldo De Mori (convener), *Michelle Becka, Antony John Baptist* (co-editors)

Part One: The Global Issue

Amazonia 4.0: An Innovative Socio-Bio-Economy for a Standing Forest

Carlos A. Nobre, Ismael Nobre, Maritta Koch-Weser

The empowerment of traditional communities that live off the forest by giving them knowledge and access to innovative technologies will promote an increase of social capital and thereby produce a change of behaviour leading to community development. If the communities produce better produce, they will obtain, first, access to markets and partnerships with businesses and investors and, second, the consolidation of a bio-economy of a standing forest that is preserved, since it will be proof that standing forests are worth more than the benefits arising from deforestation. The Amazonia 4.0 project has two components: the Creative Laboratory of Amazonia as a tool to train communities to add value to the cupuaçu-cacao chain, and the Rainforest Business School to design a new field of business knowledge for a new generation of specialists.

The tropical forests of Amazonia exist where the dry season is relatively short, normally less than three months long. Very wet and with a dense canopy, this forest reduces vulnerability to fires caused by lightning. The leaf litter and biomass in general have a high water content and the air is very humid, and the rainfall pattern and the hydrological cycles also make this region of South America different from other regions and produce a biomass with a very low level of flammability.

Nevertheless this long-term ecological balance is being gradually affected by the simultaneous combined impact of three human-induced factors of change[1]: (i) global warming, which has not only produced an increase of 1.5o C across the whole basin, but is also causing more frequent severe droughts across the whole of the Amazon basin – for example, among the most extreme droughts observed in the last 120 years were those of 2005 and 2010; (ii) deforestation in the region is increasing the surface temperature in deforested areas by 1o-3o C, and also reduced the recycling of water by vegetation; and (iii) the combination of increased surface temperatures, more extreme droughts and constant fires caused by human agency are transforming a forest previously resistant to fires into a biome more vulnerable to fires. This has led to a science-based concern that the Amazon rainforest may not be far from a tipping point at which it becomes a savannah. For example, if these three human-caused vectors continue to operate uninterrupted for the next few decades, more than 50% of the remaining forest may be turned into tropical savannah.

In the past the Amazon region sparked the greed and imagination of the Portuguese colonisers; they went deep into the forest in search of gold, silver and spices,[2] and as they encountered the unknown ointments, essences, leaves and fruits were discovered and a new range of possibilities emerged as the value of the standing forest was recognised. However, during the last 50 years the deforestation of the rainforest has produced environmental conflicts and concern on the part of the world scientific community.[3]

One of the of the principal factors in change of this magnitude is regional deforestation. It is estimated that if the deforestation rates across the basin as a whole exceed 20% to 25% of the total forest area, an irreversible process of savannisation may begin.[4] Rather than being a theoretical projection based on simulations of climate models of the impacts of human-induced change vectors (such as analysed in Nobre et al., 2016), the great concern comes from the observations of an increase of three to four weeks in the length of the dry season in the centre-south of the Amazon region since 1980.[5] The length of the dry season is the most critical element in differentiating the biosphere of the tropical forest from that of the tropical savannah. If the length of the dry season exceeds four months, the forest will be gradually transformed into a drier tropical savannah. This could represent CO2 emissions of 200-300 billion tonnes, since the tropical savannah (*cerrado*, as it is known in Brazil) stores much less carbon as compared with the tropical forest. And the delay in the start of the rainy season and the consequent increase in length of the dry season is even greater in heavily deforested areas in the south of Amazonas state.[6]

Despite all this, over three centuries the Amazon region has been on a journey in search of its economic vocation, and after going through the rubber cycle and the advent of industrialisation, there is reason to think that its economic potential can awaken now at the beginning of the 21st century with the arrival of new technologies and new processes implanted as a result of the fourth wave of industrialisation.

I. Amazonia 4.0: in search of an innovative sustainable path

It is a matter of urgency that we pose the question whether and how we can still avoid the tipping-point and maintain the Amazon forest. We can glimpse two future scenarios, to a great degree opposed and distinct, for development in the Amazon region: an ideal sustainable scenario of utopian development focused on the value of biodiversity plus zero deforestation after 2030, or a fragmented dystopic scenario of continuing intensive development of resources with an increase in deforestation.[7]

The structure of the Amazonia 4.0 programme seeks a sustainable course that can avoid the imminent tipping-point of the Amazon region, which in terms of time is 'right in front of our noses', i.e. a few decades. Collectively, the Amazon countries and the whole planet must look for spaces for a solution, including forest restoration and an innovative bio-economy based on the forest.[8] This is the main idea behind the so-called Amazonia 4.0 proposal or 'Amazonia Third Way'.[9]

For decades the debate about the development of the Amazon region was divided into two opposed visions of land use: on the one hand (let us call it 'the First Way') the vision of reserving large areas of the Amazon forests to preserve biodiversity and, on the other (we'll call it the 'the Second Way'), the vision of development based on the intensive exploitation of natural resources, principally through agriculture, energy and mining.

The Amazonia 'Third Way' initiative proposes creating an innovative alternative to these two opposed visions by implementing a strategy called Amazonia 4.0. The idea of this 'disruptive' initiative is based on new opportunities for research, technology and learning to value and protect the Amazonian ecosystems and meet the needs of the local populations, the indigenous communities and traditional populations, who are their guardians.

The aim is to develop a 'green economy' that is fair and socially inclusive, based on the forest's rich biodiversity and making use of the value of nature through sustainable products of standing tropical forests and rivers flowing from this region.

Keeping the forest standing is essential for climate stability and to avoid a tipping point into the creation of a savannah, which will very probably occur in the near future (three to five decades) if we do not succeed in reducing deforestation to zero and restoring large areas of rainforest.

The pillars of a bio-economy of standing forests and flowing rivers, based on biodiversity [10] can be summarised as follows:

- The use of biological and bio-mimetic assets in a sustainable way with the use of modern technologies;
- Just appreciation of traditional knowledge;
- Development that is socially inclusive and ecologically correct;
- A just and equitable sharing of the proceeds;
- A series of applications ranging from value chains of non-timber biodiversity products to cutting-edge genetic resources;
- Restoration of a large proportion of deforested areas to replace low-productivity cattle with native forests and agro-ecological systems.

To operationalise this innovative transformation into development based on knowledge, the concept of 'Amazonia 4.0' is being introduced to add the economic potential of Amazonian socio-biodiversity to the new technologies and possibilities emerging from the Fourth Industrial Revolution. This means the widespread use of modern technologies in the industrial revolution currently in progress – a fusion of digital technologies, bio-technology and materials science. This new process drives 'innovative ecosystems', the planned interactions of (1) advanced knowledge, both scientific and traditional, (2) new types of businesses and consumers and (3) new forms of production and intelligent equipment introduced by the Fourth Industrial Revolution.

II. Amazonia 4.0: Strategies to develop local capacities

The aim of the Amazonia 4.0 project is development genuinely structured by and for the communities, by means of the building of capacities in the Amazonian populations to lead, create and manage a bio-economy of the standing forest and flowing rivers. To this end our project is creating two interdependent mechanisms of capacity development, (i) **Amazonian Creative Laboratories** (ACLs) and (ii) **the Rainforest Business School**.

(i) Amazonian Creative Laboratories

The aim of Amazonian Creative Laboratories is to make possible an alternative to the model of expanding extractivist agriculture, which produces low income and little added value, in the form of state-of-the-art solutions that add value to existing value chains, based on biodiversity, and to explore new opportunities including even high technologies such as genomics and biomimetics.

ACLs seek to increase local capacity-building, with attributions of intellectual property rights and case-by-case experimentation on a collection of unique and economically competitive products, and projects to increase local income through a bio-economy that is inclusive, vibrant and powerful. These laboratories are currently being set up for three value-chains, cupuaçu-cacao, Brazil nuts and fine cooking oils, and one of these involves genomics.

Capacity-building exercises are being planned for various local communities in Amazonia with the cupuaçu-cacao ACL. Specifically, there are four communities that will receive the first capacity-building programmes, representing the broad range of the diversity of forest peoples: Amabela, the Rural Association of Women producers of Cupuaçu of Belterra, Pará; Arapiuns-Tapajós Sustainable Development Reserve, Santarém, Pará; Quilombo Moju, municipality of Moju Miri, Pará; and the river-dweller community of the River Acará, Pará.

The ACLs have a twofold objective: on the one hand they are disruptive of the 'business as usual' model, creatively combining local knowledge of biodiversity with production methods, equipment and market tendencies, and the most recent technologies of the Fourth Industrial Revolution made available at local and regional level. Some of the many examples of these technologies are intelligent manufacturing, automation with advanced sensors and dedicated computing; bio-sensors for quality analysis, equipment from the Internet of Things and data cloud; 3D printing; portable genomic sequencers; electronic microscopes, virtual and augmented reality for training and technical assistance; improved logistics with cargo drones; broadband connectivity; electricity provided by solar photo-voltaic systems; complete traceability of products through QR codes and microchip technologies; direct connection between producers and consumers through smartphone apps and social media to access marketing and personalise products, etc.

At the same time, they act as testbeds to discover and develop new products, processes and activities as they emerge from the interaction of specialists along the value chain and of innovative entrepreneurs in two-way interaction with local populations and traditional knowledge. In field workshops organised by the ACLs – which will take place in communities of forest peoples, towns and also on the campuses of regional universities – the participants will acquire new knowledge and will have means and incentives to increase their creativity, bringing their own inputs, biological assets, processing skills, practices and references. They will be enabled to combine their inherent knowledge with new learning and tools for the innovative and participatory development of products. The ACLs will be developed with the adequate combination of advanced biology laboratories, specialists in all aspects of value chains, high technology innovation hubs and laboratories from Brazil and other Amazon countries, and other parts of the world.

The ACLs connect directly with the Rainforest Business School (see section ii below), bringing innovative concepts and case studies for its curriculum. The capacity-building activities of the ACLs will take place 'on the campus' of Amazonian universities in order to increase the interest of students (undergraduates, graduates and post-graduates), professors and researchers in the development of bio-industries of varying degrees of complexity, through all the segments of the value chains. In this context the lecturers and researchers will also be systematically challenged to identify and fill knowledge gaps in the model of a bio-economy based on standing forests.

Operational aspects. With an eye to serving rural communities far from large urban centres and disseminating knowledge, we are designing ACLs as field laboratories operating in tents or on floating platforms, bringing together multi-disciplinary expertise in science, technology, business, logistics and legal issues. Before defining the training activities of the ACLs in the field, we shall check the interests of the communities and design the training programmes in conjunction with them. While a particular ACL will have a core content, the ACL team will adapt research, methods, tools, instruments and findings to suit the interests and the cultural, social and economic conditions of the users of the laboratory. The ACLs will be self-sufficient in energy and internet connectivity so that they can offer the capacity to carry out a variety of tests and research, materials processing and communication. As an ACL moves from one community to another, it will promote an ecosystem of sustainability and innovation for the joint creation of solutions and applications, acting as an interface for the exchange of learning and practices between communities and between communities and researchers.

(ii) The Rainforest Business School

New, sustainable businesses require innovative business education. The world's first Rainforest Business School (RBS) is being planned to shape a new field of business knowledge for a new generation of specialists. The RBS's priority will be to serve local people, industry and the business community and those who administer public programmes and policies, specialised business ventures of civil society connected with the sustainable management of forests and fisheries, and MBA students. It will cover scientific topics relating to products and value chains, market mechanisms, socio-cultural, legal and political issues. The ACLs will operate as field laboratories for the RBS in various places.

The core aim of the Rainforest Business School is to develop an interdisciplinary curriculum for doing business in tropical forests, with proper emphasis, not only on the technical and business aspects, but also on an understanding of and respect for environmental safeguards, and for the intellectual property and rights and cultures of the local communities.

Curriculum Development. The Amazon bio-economy remains small and incidental for the moment because of the lack of professionalism, business skills and knowledge that would make it possible to add value to local products based on biodiversity and political and financial support to the sector. There is a need for more ambitious socio-economic models to allow for the growth of sustainable and profitable business ventures at the level of the local community, together with the development of industrial products.

One of the main tasks of the current initial stage of development of the RBS at the State University of Amazonas is the formulation of the key components of the basic curriculum for a bio-economy based on a standing Amazon forest and flowing rivers covering, among other topics: (1) products, markets and industrial uses, for example, fruit, fibres, nuts, oils, perfumes, colorants, vegetables, pharmaceuticals, production systems based on the forest, fisheries, etc; (2) the development of models of bio-economy for communities; (3) institutional, political and legal determinants; and (4) opportunities for high technology such as genomics and biomimetics.

Curriculum development will be modular. To a great extent it can be based on case studies (for example, bio business ventures) and experiments carried out via the ACL components. Learning can be derived from traditional and indigenous production systems. In addition, a wealth of materials spread across a wide range of organisations can be made available by businesses, development projects and academic institutions.

As a key element, and taking as a teaching model the Harvard Business School, local socio-economic case studies should be carried out in the sample communities and/or small sub-regions in different Amazonian states. On the basis of experiments with existing businesses and bio-economic potential, more detailed studies will support the development of local bio-economic income, together with science-based recommendations for sustainable production systems and for the development of associated local infrastructure – energy, water quality, sanitation, storage, processing, communication, transport and marketing.

Curriculum development can speed up if various academic institutions join forces and develop components in parallel. The Rainforest Business School is being set up topic by topic. The modules will be designed and made accessible in forms that allow them to be used selectively, for example, within specific ecosystems or in particular industry or market sectors. As soon as particular modules are ready, they can be brought into use and made available to teachers and students. We have got off to a modest start, and work on the first modules has already begun, but we hope it will snowball, with the next stages evolving fast.

The Rainforest Business School is planned as a physical campus, centred on the Manaus campus of the State University of Amazonas (UEA Manaus), but also offering specialised tuition at the University of São Paulo (USP), and with a 'virtual campus' and content provider through its website *Rainforest Business School Online*, currently under construction. This 'campus' can grow as there is take-up by other teaching institutions – business schools and other academic institutions interested in adding 'rainforest business' to their curriculum. Teaching and curriculum modules will be made available to participating universities in Brazil, other Amazonian countries and also in other places. The RBS 'campus' will include tablets and apps that will give students and rainforest entrepreneurs free 'open code' access. Such an approach offers unprecedented opportunities to progress and share knowledge about sustainable rainforest businesses.

Conclusions

It is becoming increasingly urgent to find an innovative development model for the Amazon region that will preserve the wealth of biodiversity and translate the potential resources of the countless land and water ecosystems into a new bio-economy based on a standing forest and flowing, healthy rivers, an economy that is socially inclusive and combines scientific discoveries and traditional knowledge in a intelligent way. This in essence is the central aim of the Amazonia 4.0 project. This seeks to demonstrate, through its capacity-building strategy - the Amazonia Creative Laboratories and the Rainforest Business School – that it really is viable to implement a series of decentralised 'sustainable and innovative ecosystems' with the aim of adding value – that is, generating income, creating prosperity, social inclusion, empowerment and a better quality of life – to the products of the immense biodiversity of the Amazon.

To sum up, we have to find a development model that 'saves the heart of Mother Earth', in the words of the Yanomami leader Davi Kopenawa. A new paradigm of sustainable development for the rainforests must have an innovative bio-economy based on science, in other words, a solution based on Nature, meaning standing forests and flowing rivers 'to add value to the heart of the forest',[11] with appropriate policies and activities for capacity-building with the local communities.

Translated by Francis McDonagh

Notes

1. Carlos A. Nobre - Gilvan Sampaio, Laura S. Borma, Juan Carlos Castilla-Rubio and Manoel Cardoso, 'Land-use and climate change risks in the Amazon and the need of a novel sustainable development paradigm', PNAS 113, 10759-10768, (2016) [https://www.pnas.org/content/113/39/10759; https://doi.org/10.1073/pnas.1605516113].
2. Samuel Benchimol, Amazônia: um pouco-antes e além-depois, 2nd rev. ed., Manaus, 2010.
3. Augusto de la Torres - John Nash - Pablo Fajnzylber, Desenvolvimento com menos carbono: respostas da América Latina ao desafio da mudança climática, Rio de Janeiro, 2010.
4. Thomas E. Lovejoy and Carlos A. Nobre, 'Amazon Tipping Point', Science Advances 4.2 (2018), eaat2340 [DOI: 10.1126/sciadv.aat2340].
5. Rong Fu, Lei Yin, Wenhong Li, Paola A. Arias, Robert E. Dickinson, Lei Huang, Sudip Chakraborty, Katia Fernandes, Brant Liebmann, Rosie Fisher, Ranga B. Myneni, 'Increased dry-season length over southern Amazonia in recent decades and its implication for future climate projection', PNAS (November 5, 2013) 110 (45), 18110-18115; https://doi.org/10.1073/pnas.1302584110.
6. Argemiro Teixeira Leite-Filho, Verônica Yameê de Sousa Pontes and Marcos Heil Costa, 'Effects of deforestation on the onset of the rainy season and the duration of dry spells in Southern Amazonia', Journal of Geophysical Research: Atmospheres 124, (2019), 5268-5281 [https://doi.org/10.1029/2018 JD029537].
7. Ana Paula Dutra Aguiar, Ima Célia Guimarães Vieira, Talita Oliveira Assis, Eloi L. Dalla-Nora, Peter Mann Toledo, Roberto Araújo Oliveira Santos-Junior, Mateus Batistella, Andrea Santos Coelho, Elza Kawakami Savaget, Luiz Eduardo Oliveira Cruz Aragão, Carlos Afonso Nobre and Jean Pierre H. Ometto, 'Land use change emission scenarios: anticipating a forest transition process in the Brazilian Amazon', Global Change Biology 22, (2016), 1821-1840 [https://doi.org/10.1111/gcb.13134].
8. Thomas E. Lovejoy and Carlos A. Nobre, 'Amazon Tipping Point: Last chance for action', Science Advances 5 (2019), eaba2949 [DOI: 10.1126/sciadv.aba2949].
9. Ismael Nobre and Carlos A. Nobre, 'The Amazonia Third Way Initiative: the role of technology to unveil the potential of a novel tropical biodiversity-based economy', in: Louis C. Loures (ed.), Land Use - Assessing the Past, Envisioning the Future [Open Access Book], IntechOpen, 2019; Luís Roberto Barroso and Patrícia Perrone Campos Mello, 'How to save the Amazon: Why the forest has more value standing than cut down' Revista de Direito da Cidade, 12 (2), 2020, 449-503. DOI: 10.12957/rdc.2020.50890.
10. www.amazoniaquatropontozero.org
11. A famous phrase of the late Bertha Becker, a geographer from the Federal university of Rio de Janeiro, who inspired us to search for sustainable routes for the Amazon region.

The Ecological Crisis and Tropical Forest Ecosystems: Cases from Africa, Asia, and Melanesia

Nicole Bernex

In the last 10,000 years, deforestation due to human causes has generated severe impacts. It is necessary to specify the current context and its dynamics in the tropical forests of Africa and Asia, before analysing the contribution of those ecosystems to human well-being, the impacts of their degradation on ecosystems, and their direct consequences on the growth of poverty for millions of people. Finally, it is also necessary to recognize not only the social and economic nature of the ecological crisis, but also that its eco-ethical essence allows for strategies to increase the resilience of ecosystems and the communities that depend on them.

In the memory of the planet, the history of the ecological crisis is discovered in small and large traces, impacts, adjustments, changes; a crisis amplified by the rhythm of continuous revolutions. Undoubtedly the first great revolution with important consequences in nature was the Neolithic revolution (8500 BCE), with the domestication of animals and plants, the consequent sedentarization, and the first major impacts on the Huang He and Yangtze river basins. Sadowski recognizes the positives and negatives of the Neolithic revolution, especially in terms of health and deforestation to gain land for cereal crops.[1] More critically, Diamond points out how those regions of the Mediterranean and Asia lost their forests and today enjoy only poor scrub and deserts, all because, "its woodlands were cleared for agriculture, or cut to obtain construction timber, or burned as firewood or for manufacturing plaster."[2] These processes created new dynamics of soil degradation. The age of metals, copper, bronze, and iron accentuated these changes in natural landscape.

Throughout the millennia and centuries, human interventions have diversified in the management of the forest and vegetation cover, flora and fauna, soil and water, and it must be recognized that all human intervention, without exception, means an impact on the ecosystems where it occurs and on the societies that inhabit them. The ecological crisis that began in the Neolithic era has lasted, become more complex through the rate of technological revolutions and has been reinforced throughout the entire planet. One of the characteristics of this crisis is the degradation and deterioration of ecosystems, seeing the loss of their services; another of its characteristics is its human face.

I. Ecosystems, complex systems

For more than five decades, numerous scientific studies have been carried out on ecosystems, as well as on complex systems theory and social systems theory. Although there are more and more dialogues between the sciences, often those dialogues do not integrate sciences such as history, archaeology, geography, agronomy, engineering, the arts, and others. Consequently, the interdisciplinary effort is truncated. Likewise, certain teams, voluntarily betting on interdisciplinarity, remain within a juxtaposition of crossed approaches and perspectives. They do not take the time to pose the real questions or to construct interdisciplinary methodologies.

How could ancient civilizations reach the level of knowledge to build entire cities, tame the slopes, understand the links between soil and subsoil, manage water, know the currents of the seas and rivers, and plan their territory? Key were the connections with the water, the sun, the sky and its stars, the winds, the reins, the mountains, the forests, the plants and animals, and the sea. From the continuous observation of the different elements of nature, many societies discovered how much they depended on nature, and this knowledge led them to care for, respect, and sacralise nature, "mother-nature", to consider it as a living bring, fruitful and protective. Today, science calls this mother-nature, this factory of unique life that works continuously and provides its services freely to all living communities "ECOSYSTEM." Since 2001, the contributions of the Millennium Ecosystem Assessment have made it possible to understand that the current modus vivendi, the growth of populations, the diversification of their demands, and changes in land use, are translated into a continuous reduction of ecosystem services, and therefore the diversity of life.

Four groups of ecosystem services are recognized: support services (or habitat services), which are the basis for producing the other ecosystem services; regulatory services, which regulate processes in ecosystems; supply services, which provide material benefits such as wood, food, and fresh water; and cultural services, which provide non-material benefits (Figure 1).[3]

Figure 1. Ecosystem services

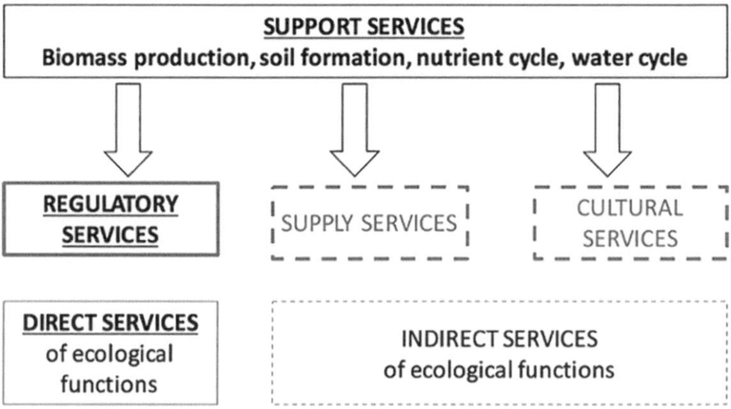

Source: Nicole Bernex, GWP: 5; 2016 [figure translated by translator].

Regulatory services are performed directly by ecosystems based on their functions. Among others, there are the regulation of water renewal, biological purification and control, erosion control, carbon sequestration, climate regulation, and soil conservation. When one of those services is degraded, the quality of the environment is degraded and human well-being is affected. Reversing this situation means a high cost in science – technology and innovation and it is it not always possible within our current state of knowledge.

Currently, nature is no longer the "great teacher" of millions of people living in cities, who ignore the vital connectivity between elements: rivers and fish, forests and pollinators, air-water and soil, the rhythms of soil-evapotranspiration and vegetation, etc. The degradation of ecosystem services by the actions of societies not only means a loss of health for ecosystems, but is also expressed by a significant loss of human health and the increase in vulnerability of all societies at a planetary level.

The scientific super-specialization limits the investigation of the complex connectivity of the triple dimension of ecosystems (atmospheric, surface, and underground) and of the major connectors, water, energy, soil, and biodiversity. Likewise, the urban person ceases to be the great connector that they were in other times when they lived within the rhythm of nature, learning to treasure the services for mutual benefit. For some fifty years, unprecedented rural migrations, vertiginous urbanization coupled with the deterioration of education programs, have alienated urban communities from nature. In general, they are unaware of the benefits that ecosystems provide them and the degradation of the services that they themselves generate.

II. The forest ecosystems of the tropics of Africa, Asia, and Melanesia

Forests make up 31% of the earth's surface; more than half of those formations are located in the intertropical zone, between the tropics of Cancer and Capricorn, densifying around the equatorial line. If there are differences in climate history and magnitude between the primary forests of the Amazon and Congo basins, there is no doubt that they have a common DNA, the memory of the ancient continent of Gondwana, and the similarities between them predominate. They enjoy great integrity and significant natural regeneration; they benefit from their complementary position between two hemispheres; their main rivers have huge amounts of water, with the average flow of the Amazon River being 225,000 m^3/s and that of the 41,800 m^3/s. At the same time, a large part of the population living in these low-density forests do not have access to safe water for life. The two most important tropical rainforests on the planet have a long history of occupation, little known in the case of the Amazon rainforest for about 12,000 years; better known in the case of the Congo jungle.

Though both forests suffer continuous anthropic interventions, there is no comparison with the tropical forests of Asia and Melanesia.

All the tropical forests of Africa, Asia, and Melanesia constitute areas of extraordinary concentrations of biodiversity, systematized into six vegetation zones by the Food and Agriculture Organization (FAO) of the United Nations, namely the tropical rain forest, the tropical moist deciduous forest, the tropical dry forest, the tropical shrubland, the tropical desert, and tropical mountain systems. The interplay of altitude, latitude and exposure, local climatic variability, continentality, or insularity explain the fabulous diversity and multiplication of minor ecological zones.

If the Amazon basin is the largest in the world (7,413,827 km^2), it is inhabited by only about 34 million people, while the Congo basin (3,700,000 km^2) has more than 136,000,000 inhabitants. Table 1 highlights the characteristics of certain countries, their contrasts, and highlights certain worrying aspects. In the Congo basin, in all countries, the total area occupied by agriculture is less than the total area covered by forests. In Cameroon where the pressures to expand agricultural frontiers are high, it reaches 1/5 of the forest cover; in the Democratic Republic of the Congo (DRC), 1/6; and, in the Central African Republic, 1/39. The growth of the population of Madagascar, the generalization of slash and burn in the eastern tropical forests, together with the continuous deforestation of the central plateau, imply the rapid retreat of the forests and loss of all the biodiversity in this insular space.

This situation of tropical rainforest stress is very common on the southwestern coasts of India, the lowlands of the coasts of Southeast Asia, the Philippines, and most of the Malay Archipelago. Most of these countries are characterized by very large populations, high density, remnants of old growth forests, continuous deforestation, and at the same time, for a decade, a net increase in forest area due to plantations. India, Thailand, and the Philippines are the three countries whose area occupied by crops exceeds that occupied by forests. Myanmar and Vietnam follow this trend.

Table 1: Some general characteristics of the studied countries[4]

	Population 2019	Total area of the country	Total area covered by forests	Total area occupied by agriculture	Total area occupied by scrubs
Central African Republic	Inhabitants	km²	Mha	Mha	Mha
	4,745,190	623,000	51.1	1.31	10.3
Democratic Republic of Congo	86,790,570	2,345,000	169.0	27.5	10.2
Republic of the Congo	5'380,510	342,000	21.8	3.44	3.8
Cameroon	25,876,380	475,000	35.5	7.36	3.24
Gabon	2,172,580	267,700	23.4	1.33	*927.0kha
South Sudan	11,062,110	620,000	24.4	3.4	29.1
Madagascar	26,969,310	587,000	15.7	8.76	36.9
India	1,366,417,750	3'290,000	50.3	236.0	27.6
Indonesia	270,625,570	1'900,000	100.0	67.1	1.0
Malaysia	31,949,750	330,000	20.2	10.8	*36.0 kha
Brunei	433,296	5,765	*458kha	*66.2kha	
Myanmar	54,045,420	676,600	27.6	24.4	17.8
Thailand	62,625,580	513,000	8.4	36.3	7.0
Laos	7,062,000	236,800	9.6	4.5	10.0
Vietnam	96,462,110	331,200	27.6	24.4	17.8
Philippines	108,116,620	300,000	9.5	16.6	7.0
Papua New Guinea	8,776,110	462,840	38.2	5.7	*243kha

Table 1 & 2 source: FAO and GFW statistics; table formulation by author.

Table 2 highlights the dynamics of land use between 2001 and 2016. Differences appear between the tropical forests of Africa and those of

Asia and Melanesia. The latter have seen the acceleration of the loss of their primary forests, and therefore a greater fragmentation of their forests. However, in the countries of the Congo Basin, forest management plans are scarce while much of the tropical forests of India, Southeast Asia, the Philippines, and the Malay Archipelago have growing areas of forest plantations; parts of them being intensively managed for production purposes and others for ecosystem restoration and protection purposes.

Table 2: Forest land use by country (2001-2016)

	Old-Growth Forest		Other Tree Cover	Old-Growth Forest		Other Tree Cover	Planted Forest
	Mha	%	Mha	Mha	%	Mha	kha
Central African Republic	7.4	16	39.7	494kha	1	46.7	2.0
Democratic Republic Of Congo	105.0	52	94.7	60.8	31	138.0	60.4
Republic Of Congo	21.2	80	5.2	10.6	40	16.0	71.0
Cameroon	19.1	61	12.4	3.6	12	27.0	25.6
Gabon	22.7	92	2.0	8.0	33	16.7	30.0
South Sudan	*83.7kha	0.74	11.3	0	0	13.3	0.0
Madagascar	4.8	28	12.3	1.22	7.4	15.2	312.0
India	10.2	26	28.6	2.31	6.7	32.1	12,000.0
Indonesia	93.8	58	66.8	30.3	19	128.0	4,950.0
Malaysia	15.9	54	13.5	1.5	5.3	27.1	1,970.0
Brunei	*431kha	82	*97.9kha	*161kha	30	*368 kha	0.3
Myanmar	14.0	33	28.8	2.9	7.1	38.0	944.0
Thailand	5.9	30	14.0	1.7	8.8	17.6	3,900.0
Laos	8.3	44	10.8	1.2	5.0	0.0	113.0
Vietnam	6.7	41	9.8	*296kha	1.8	16.1	3,600.0
Philippines	4.6	25	14.0	*357kha	1.9	18.0	1,250.0
Papua New Guinea	32.6	76	10.3	13.0	30	29.9	0.0

III. Tropical forests' ecosystem services and their degradation

Forest ecosystems provide a wide range of essential services called ecosystem services. All human beings depend on forests, some more and others less. In other words, the well-being of humanity depends on the balance of the life cycles of basic ecosystem services. By degrading them, we affect atmospheric and ocean currents, affect the general circulation of the planet, induce local climate change, and accelerate global climate change.

Forests help moderate extreme weather events, droughts and floods, increase evapotranspiration, and contribute to climate stability, air and water purification; forests help to maintain the global hydrological cycle, the carbon cycle and the nutrient cycle, increase percolation and facilitate the renewal of aquifers, regulate the flow of rivers and streams, stabilize the soil and protect it against water and wind erosion.

Likewise, tropical forests provide various services, they provide a habitat for numerous species of plants, animals, pollinators, and natural predators of pests. They are home to local populations that live off them in many regions. They provide them with food, medicinal plants, resins, fuels (firewood) and wood, potential and commercial resources, among others. Each forest is unique and has its own value. Mangrove forests contain an enormous density of fish, crustaceans, oysters, and other communities; the moabi, iconic of the Guinean-Congolese forest, is a tree of thousands of uses, highly valued in carpentry, food, and pharmacopoeia. In the tropical rain forests of India, sandalwood, sacred trees, teak, and sisu (in English Indian rosewood). In the lowland rainforests of Malaysia and Indonesia, very tall, melliferous trees, the tualangs, trees that link the earth to the sky, predominate. Peatlands in tropical rainforests are exceptional habitats and resources. In the Congo Basin, the Cuvette peat bog, the world's largest complex with 14.5 million hectares of hardwood and palm trees, is characterized by high densities of lowland gorillas, bonobos, chimpanzees, African forest elephants, and dwarf crocodiles.

All these ecosystems provide food security, quality of life; they constitute unique places to visit and to know. They allow jobs to be created and are sources of eco-tourist cultural activities, due to the diversification of their landscapes. They contain the worldview of diverse indigenous peoples, strengthening their identity. Thus, the Bantu believe that the local rosewood trees contain the spirits of the ancestors and protect them.

The multifunctionality of the forest allows us to understand the importance of each ecosystem service and how it constitutes the basis of economic, social, and environmental sustainability. However, at present, forest ecosystems are threatened by various human activities, by the loss of identity with nature, by the growing ignorance that mostly urban populations have of ecosystems and their services, by changes in their customs of consumption, the growing overconsumption and waste of water, energy, food, discarded items, and resources. Living off the backs of the forests, wetlands and bogs, and riparian vegetation makes us increasingly vulnerable. All security decreases: food security obtained freely from the forest (honey, fruits, meat), water security offered freely by the forest, economic security due to the multiple opportunities for harvesting and selling honey, nuts, fruits, wild meat, and fish to local populations.

The loss of old growth forests, their fragmentation not only degrades ecosystems and their services, but also accelerates climate change. Table 3 presents the loss of tree cover and its CO2 emissions. In 2019, in the DRC, the loss of 1.22 million hectares of tree cover meant 512 million tons of CO2 emissions. Cameroon follows with 45.5 million tons. In Asia, the loss of tree cover stands out in Indonesia, Myanmar, and Malaysia with 187, 116, and 97 million tons of CO2 emissions. Tropical forests are exceptional natural carbon sinks. The decrease in this forest carbon stock has a direct impact on global climate change.

Table 3: Tree cover, loss, and equivalent CO2 emissions

COUNTRIES	2010		2019	
	Tree Cover Area	Percentage of Tree Area/ Total Area	Loss of Tree Cover	Equivalent CO2 Emissions
	Mha	%	kha	Mt
Central African Republic	47.2	76	49.0	15.5
Democratic Republic of Congo	198.0	85	1220.0	512.0
Republic of Congo	26.6	78	73.8	26.8

COUNTRIES	2010		2019	
	Tree Cover Area	Percentage of Tree Area/ Total Area	Loss of Tree Cover	Equivalent CO2 Emissions
Cameroon	30.4	66	120.0	45.5
Gabon	24.7	93	28.5	12.1
South Sudan	13.3	21	3.8	*908kt
Madagascar	16.4	28	254.0	80.8
India	31.3	11	115.0	43.5
Indonesia	93.8	50	324.0	187.0
Malaysia	20.3	87	193.0	97.1
Brunei	*529kha	92	*1.17 kha	*500kt
Myanmar	40.1	61	297.0	116.0
Thailand	19.1	37	129.0	50.0
Vietnam	14.5	50	150.0	50.9
Philippines	13.2	62	48.2	19.1
Papua New Guinea	42.6	93	91.2	51.5

Source: FAO and GFW statistics; table formulation by author.

We all depend on forests, some more and others less. The degradation of tropical forests has a growing impact on the quality of life of all the inhabitants of the planet.

Along with the expansion of agriculture, industrial logging is the main factor in the degradation and deforestation of African and Asian rainforests, especially selective logging, charcoal collection, and the development of road infrastructure. These represent some of the most important causes of acceleration of forest degradation. In the Congo Basin, much of the forestry activity is carried out illegally behind the back of the state. Combined with this are the forgery of documents, plundering of native groups in situ, corruption, military conflicts, etc.

Informality and illegality characterize a large part of the activities that take place in the forest by those not born in the forest, among others, the poaching of wild animals such as the so-called ecosystem engineers (elephants) for their ivory, rhinos for their horns, tiger, leopards and other cats for their skins, and various species of crocodiles for their hides. It should be noted that, despite its better regulation, hunting is much more important in Asia due to its huge urban market in food and traditional medicine. The smuggling of wild animals is endless, from insects, small lizards, birds, monkeys, and ornamental fish.

Forests are favourite areas for exploitation and smuggling of resources, among other things minerals, for example, cobalt in the DRC, sapphires in Madagascar, jade in Burma, gold in the Congo, Indonesia, Papua New Guinea, exploited without the protection of adult and child workers or ecosystems. The tropical forests of Africa, Asia, and Melanesia are spaces of free movement for all groups that carry out illegal activities of money laundering, organized crime, and human trafficking. They are practically "free territories."

Likewise, the architecture of family power can become one of the causes of degradation of tropical rain forests, such as the Widjaja family in Indonesia, with its international paper and pulp industry, its coal mines and its oil palm and acacia plantations for productive purposes, affecting deep peat swamps in the province of Riau.

Human interventions denying life degrade both ecosystems and the quality of interrelationships between actors in the same territory, limiting social peace. The loss of quality of ecosystems and their services increases the poverty of the inhabitants of those regions. Without ecosystem health, there is no human health.

Conclusions

One of the justifications for deforestation is the poverty of the populations that have lived in situ since time immemorial and of the populations that live in the forest within their direct area of influence, populations that require food, water, and materials provided by the forest for their daily lives. In reality, it is the opposite, in the past when they were more numerous, those populations received everything freely from the forest. Today, as those forests have been fragmented, they have lost a large part of their biodiversity that guaranteed food security and health to the indigenous populations. The pollution of their waters and the increase in their climatic variability made their populations more vulnerable. The free gifts of nature have no replacement.

Certainly, ahead of the known networks of organized crime and corruption at a global level, there is the severe lack of education that largely explains the global ecological crisis and that of tropical forest ecosystems. Reversing it is taking the path of building an ecosocial resilience. Goodwill and the increasing numbers of studies, programs, and investments for the restoration of ecosystems and helping the poor are not enough to achieve a decent life. It is about reconnecting with nature, learning gratuitousness, and embarking on the path of a global diplomacy of education and health along with a culture of care (*Laudato sí*), within the framework of an eco-ethics and alter-ethics.

Translated by Thia Cooper

Notes

1. Ryszard F. Sadowski, Neolithic Revolution. In: P. Thompson, D. Kaplan (eds), Encyclopedia of Food and Agricultural Ethics. Dordrecht: Springer, 2017, at https://doi.org/10.1007/978-94-007-6167-4_540-1 [20 November, 2020]
2. Jared Diamond, Guns, Germs, and Steel: The Fates of Human Societies. New York London: W. W. Norton & Company, 1999, 411, at https://www.academia.edu/35388552/GUNS_GERMS_AND_STEEL_THE_FATES_OF_HUMAN_SOCIETIES_Jared_Diamond [10 October, 2020]
3. Nicole Bernex, Linking ecosystem services and water security. SDGs offer a new opportunity for integration. Global Water Partnership, Perspective Papers, 2016, 20.
4. All the forest statistics are from the FAO (http://www.fao.org/forest-resources-assessment/es/;
https://fra-data.fao.org/) and the Global Forest Watch (GFW) online platform provides data and tools for forest monitoring (https://www.globalforestwatch.org/). Population statistics come from the World Bank. (https://datos.bancomundial.org/indicator/SP.POP.TOTL)

Extractivism: A Perspective of Social Ethics

Gerhard Kruip

This contribution tries, in the first instance, to explain the frequently observed phenonemen that, in many cases, countries that are rich in raw materials are among the poorer countries, and countries that are poor in raw materials are, in contrast, among the richer ones. Following this, the neo-extractivism of Latin America will be described, with certain aspects shown specifically by using the example of Bolivia. Finally, the thesis is posited that, for a socially more just and sustainable policy for the exploitation or raw materials, targetted measures are possible, which, given the political will, could also be implemented under the present capitalist market economy system. Faced with growing environmental problems, we cannot wait for an overthrow of capitalism, which, from our present viewpoint, has to be seen as utopian.

In the area of the Amazon and the Andes region, *extractivism* contributes significantly to the growing social conflicts and the worsening of environmental problems. Worldwide, too, this is a problematic economy, which is why the following addresses the fundamentals of the issue.

The term *extractivism*, which is little used in German, firstly defines a form of economy in which hunters and gatherers *extract* living wild animals and plants as well as their fruit from their environment, to live of them, without significantly changing this environment. In the context of colonial history this term means the exploitation of raw material by the colonialists during which the raw material that has been extracted in the primary sector by farming or mining neither remained in the colonies, nor were they refined there, but were exported as raw materials, so that very litte of the wealth that was created with them remained in their regions of origin. At most, small local elites were able to profit from them. After the end of the colonial age, too, this process remains in the form of neo-colonial structures. The term *neo-extractivism* is used, nowadays, when the governments use the raw material wealth of their countries to combat poverty and to generally grow wealth, but continue to not refine or process them themselves. While this used to be attributed, in the past, more to so called 'right' governments, this criticism is nowadays also addressed to 'left' governments.

Raw materials have played an important role in the history of humandkind. They were deciding factors in economic and cultural development and were often enough a reason for martial conflicts. The discovery of deposits of certain metals and the inventions to process them have given their names to whole ages (Bronze Age, Iron Age). With the emergence of a monetary economy the significance of precious metals increased enormously. The greed for gold was one of the main driving factors in the colonialisation of America. The export of large amounts of silver from Bolivia and Mexico led, in the 16th and 17th century, to mounting inflation in Europe. In the 19th century, coal and steel were the most important driving forces of the industrial revolution. In the 20th century, mineral oil and mineral gas were at the centre of economic and geostrategic interests and conflicts. In the process of digitalisation and transformation towards the decarbonisation of the ecnomony, rare soils and the raw materials lithium and cobal that are so important for batteries gain importance. Due to the world wide economic growth and the global increase in population, the extraction and processing of raw materials has massively increased in recent decades.This is why it should be expected that some raw materials become rare and accordingly more expensive over the next few years.[1] This is, however, not true for fossil sources of energy. To sustain a climate that supports life their use has to be drastically reduced long before their deposits are exhausted.[2] In addition not only the usage, but also the extraction of fossil sources of energy leads to such signifcant damage to the environment that means that there is some urgency to replacing them with more sustainable sources of energy, for example by using solar energy, which is often present to a large extent exactly where mineral oil and gas are extracted.

I. Why do raw material rich countries often remain poor?

While many rich industrial states, like for example Germany or Japan, are poor in natural resources, but are nevertheless very wealthy, the wealth in raw materials has turned out to be a *resource curse* for many poor countries. This is hardly surprising when the exploitation of raw materials was carried out by foreign powers, aided by colonial mechanisms. But even without such dependencies, a wealth in raw materials is not necessarily a guarantee for a positive development. This phenonem is generally called 'Dutch disease'[3], as industrial production declined in the Netherlands in the 1960s, following the discovery of large deposits of mineral gas. If a country, by exporting a lot of raw materials, achieves a foreign trade surplus, this leads to a real appreciation of its currency and thus to a loss of the ability of other domestic products to compete on national and international markets. Many of the things that used to be produced in the same country before are now being imported. This can lead to a decrease in employment which is not compensated for by the raw material sector which does not need a significant workforce. Sachs and Warner have demonstrated, with statistical methods and in a global comparison, that there is a relatively clear connection between a high proportion of raw materials in exports and low growth.[4] More recent analyses show that in particular the wealth in mineral oil fosters the continued existence or the emergence of authoritarian regimes, and leads to a stronger tendency to corruption, and to violent conflict.[5]

Countries which export raw materials are also heavily dependent on the frequently varying prices on the global market. Rising prices and the attendant rise in state income often seduce governments to high spending and those who profit from it within the country to rising consumption, without this growth really being sustainable, while dropping prices contribute to huge economic downturns and then a rising government debt. These disadvantageous effects are worsened in countries that are rich in raw materials which – like for example Venezuela in Latin America or Nigeria or Sambia in Africa – are not well governed, that is when employers are not protected from exploitation, free unions are not permitted, there is hardly any effective legislation for the protection of the environment, welfare state protection mechanisms for the unemployed and the poor are lacking, and government agencies and courts of law are corrupt, with the consequence that legislation is not really applied. Little creation of value remains in the country, too, when there are not enough qualified workers or the capital for local investment is lacking, be it because the country's elite coalition prefer to move the money that they have gained by exporting raw materials abroad, or because foreign capital holders assess the conditions for an investment in these countries to be too insecure. Frequently, mining leads to local conflict. Many civil war like conflicts are financed by the export of raw material. Thomas Pogge showed how wealthy countries and multinational companies seduce the local elites in poorer countries to exploit raw materials in such a way that it is beneficial for these elites, and the rich countries and the companies who cooperate with them, but not for the poor (raw material privilege)[6]. Of course, consumers in rich countries, but also the middle and upper levels of society in emerging countries have some responsibility for this due to their demand. It is, however, not automatically the case that the wealth in raw material necessarily leads to poverty in the great majority of the population. Much depends on whether there is good governance on a local, regional and national level. Good politics can make a difference, as shown by many examples.[7]

II. Neo-extractivism using the example of Latin America[8]

The high dependence of many Latin American countries on the export of raw materials is an inheritance from colonial times, but was also sustained since the indepence at the beginning of the 19th century in the interest of local elites, transnational companies, and rich countries in the North, especially the USA, and, in the mining sector, also Canada. The increasing discovery and extraction of mineral oil and gas, too (Mexico, Venezuela, and later also Ecuador and Bolivia) seamlessly became part of this system. Since the beginning of the 21st century, hower, when left leaning governments came into power in many countries (Hugo Chávez 1999 in Venezuela, Luis Inácio Lula da Silva 2003 in Brazil, Néstor Kirchner 2003 in Argentinia, Evo Morales 2006 in Bolivia and Rafael Correa 2002 in Ecuador) attempts were made, through higher taxes on the mining of raw materials, a direct involvement of state companies, and sometimes through the nationalisation of mining companies, to keep a larger proportion of the profit in the country. Driven by high raw material prices on the international markets, the exploitation of raw materials has increased significantly in many cases. A part of the higher state income was used for social programmes which were meant to fight poverty, but also served to legitimise the relevant governments. There are, indeed, high levels of growth in the first years of these governments, and in many countries the poverty quota did go down. It has rarely been sucessful, however, to keep a higher proportion of the value-added chain in the country, and to further develop other economic areas. The proportion of raw material exports in all exports is still, in many of these countries, over 90 per cent. This is why the term of neo-extractivism has found widespread usage. In this respect, a substantial change becomes evident. This is because the South American left strongly criticised the extractivist enclave economies in the past, while they are today defending it as an essential component for development and for combatting poverty.[9] Unfortunately, the projects of the left that were promising in the beginning in the above named countries have, for various reasons, come to dead ends, particularly dramatically so in Venezuela, the political and economic situation of which looks almost hopeless, and people are much worse off than in the times of "neoliberal" governments. Millions have left the country in the meantime.

The situation in Bolivia can be seen with cautious optimism. Evo Morales (Movimiento al Socialismo – MAS) was the first president with indigenous roots in a country in which indigenous groups make up more than half of the population.

As early as in the first year of his government he increased taxes which the companies that extracted raw materials had to pay to the state and *nationalised* extraction of mineral gas that had been privatised in 1997. Through this, and through the high price of mineral oil on the global market, government income rose dramatically and remained above government spending from 2006 to 2013.[10] The real gross national product, too, rose from 2001 to 2013, only briefly interrupted by a drop due to the financial crisis of 2009. In about the same period, the exports were also higher than the imports. It remained unchanged, however, that raw materials such as mineral gas, mineral oil, ore and metals accounted for more than 90 per cent of exports. The export diversification which was aimed for, which would have brought with it a greater independence of the global market, has not been achieved. Only 7 per cent of exports were refined products.

Since 2000, and then chiefly during the boom from 2006 to 2013, lowering the poverty rote from 62,1 per cent to 26 per cent in 2013 was however successful, which constitutes a big success of the social measures that were launched by Morales. Since then, however, it has only very slightly sunk to 23,1 per cent in 2018.[11]

Results look less good when focusing on questions of the protection of the environment. Many of the spoil heaps from earlier mining, particularly those that are significantly contaminated with heavy metals, remain unsecured. There are great doubts as to whether the companies that exploit the raw materials and the even less controlled mining cooperatives as well as the illegal mining in decommissioned mines really do keep to environmental legislation, which is not very strict in the first place. Especially the illegal extraction of gold with the aid of mercury is associated with great enviornmental damage. The construction of a connecting street between the highland and the low land through the national park and indigenious protection area Isiboro-Secure (TIPNIS) triggered strong social and political protests and showed how little importance the protection of the enviornment held for Evo Morales, who in other cases always quoted his respect for mother earth. Bolivia had high hopes for its wealth in lithium that is located in the salt lake of Uyuni. Here, too, however, the mining is associated with environmental problems and it is reasonable to admit considerable doubt as to whether it will be possible to establish the production of batteries or electronic cars in the country itself.

III. Recommendations for sustainable politics for the exploitation of raw materials[12]

With non renewable resources sustainability cannot mean to only live off the interests of nature capital, as that would mean not using them at all. This is, however, ethically permissible, when future generations end up, through this, with fewer raw materials, but with other goods in return which compensate for the disadvantage, for example more efficient technology, a better infrastrtucture, better education, or more stable social and political circumstances.[13] The putting in practice of such a moderate demand for sustainability does not, as Gudynas claims, require the overcoming of capitalism.[14] Even if you think that it is plausible to hope for fundamental alternatives to capitalism, we have run out of time to wait for them. The present economic and political power structures make a turning away from capitalism a hope for a distant future. It makes much more sense to realise that, on the scale of economic systems and policies, there are, absolutely, better and worse alternatives.[15] The discourse on a *post growth society*, too, is sensible only when this also means the reduction of environmental impact, while precisely during a sensible restructuring towards sustainability the gross domestic product as the measure of all goods and services rendered will continue to grow and should grow to be able to finance these transformations. In this context, relatively concrete and easy to carry out measures can be aimed for, which I will present here in a much condensed form.

Because the exploitation of non renewable resources has a forseeable end in many countries, it is necessary to anticipate that end now. The gain from mining and from the sector of fossil fuel which at the moment yields relatively high revenues will not be a sustainable sources of income. They will only be available for a limited number of years. If you take the principle of sustainability seriously, then it does not mean the complete renounciation of the use of non renewable resources, but it demands that the income is invested for a future in which it no longer exists. From this follows, initally, that the income that is generated from them should not solely go to private companies, but that the state, through appropriate taxes and levies, has to get its rightful share. In the past this has often not been the case due to damaging complicity between private companies and the state. At the same time, it is, however, important that the regulatory framework creates incentives for private companies, so that the economic activity of companies becomes attractive. It does not always have to be the state which extracts raw materials. Often, it is unfortunately the case that state-owned companies, due to the inefficiency of bureaucracy or to corruption create less surplus for the state than private companies if they are strictly regulated and made to actually pay the taxes and levies that the law prescribes.

When the exploitation of raw materials leads to income for the state, it is necessary, finally, to reflect carefully on what they should be used for. They should, as a matter of priority, enable investments for the time after the end of raw material extraction. This is why it should mainly be used for the education of children and teenagers, as it is them who will live in post extractivist times. And from everything we know about the importance of education, it is one of the most important resources for a just and sustainable development.

Income from the extraction fo raw materials should be invested in a sustainable infrastructure of the country, particularly in the areas of traffic and communcation and an alternative energy supply (wind and sun). To avoid the Dutch disease it is very important that the founding of companies whose production serves to heighten the share of added value by processing raw material should be supported. In addition, companies should be supported that can replace foreign imports through their own products, and, even more importantly, that can diversify the exports of the country to move away from the one sided export of raw materials.

All of this means that the income from extracting non renewable raw materials should not be used for immediate consumption or short term activities, and especially not for political propaganda, which only serve the legitimisation of the party that is currently in power. Some states use the income to strongly subsidise products, for example fuel, that are made from local oil. This may serve to combat poverty, but it also involves very high spending by the states and prevents the necessary incentives to save energy and to invest into more ecological technologies. In addition, such a high degree of subsidies carries the danger of hard political protests occuring when, one day – and this day will come -the subsidies are reduced. Often, the income from the extraction of raw materials is also being used for direct social transfer payments, which might, from the perspective of a necessary fight against poverty, be sensible for the moment. Nevertheless, the sustainability of transfer payments finally depends on whether jobs are created and companies make profit in the long run, and pay their taxes.

As the exploitation of raw materials always goes hand in hand with ecological damage, and most of the time also with social problems, particularly the pollution of water and soil, the short term economic advantages should not be seen to have a higher priority than the long term social and ecological damages. The ecological criteria do not only serve to preserve a certain environment, but chiefly serve to not impair the life and the wellbeing of future generations. In addition, it is the task of the state to remove damages to the environment of the past (for example, spoil heaps from past mining), or to make the companies that caused the damage to make relevant reparations. A special case is the highly problematic extraction of gold in Brazil, Peru, Bolivia and Ecuador, for which high amounts of mercury are used, which endanger, both in the short and in the medium term, the health of the population and the environmental balance. Here, it is urgently necessary to take effective measures to forbid the use of this deadly poision.

Often, it can not be avoided that the extraction of raw material comes with disadvantages for some social groups, while other sectors and society as a whole have important advantages. In such cases, extraction can be legitimate if – and only if! – there are appropriate compensations for the disadvantaged, and if their fundamental rights are respected. Often, such compensations are not guaranteed, and the fundamental rights, particularly with regards to political participation and the right to be heard, for example according to the ILO convention 169 are not sufficiently guaranteed. This is when compensations depend on the often very low power of negotiation of the groups concerned. A fairer compensation has to be the task and the intention of the whole society and its current government. The same is true for a fair division of the income from mining between the different sectors of society as well as to regions and parts of the country. It is of the utmost importance that an excessive profit of some regions is prevented.

Non renewable resources do not have to be a curse. Rather, the advantages and disadvantages depend on the ability of the government to plan the raw materials sector well and to efficiently look after the income. This presupposes that the states overcome its institutional weaknesses and that political culture keeps developing. The central problem lies in a lack of real political participation of citizens, particular of the indigenous groups who are particularly concerned, the political processes and the lack of political will to truly achieve such an inclusion of all in a new society. The possibility to participate in the political process should not only be guaranteed for parties, but also to the same degree for organisations of indigenous peoples, for small scale entrepreneurs and farmers, as well as for environmental organisations, churches, youth organisations and many more.

IV. A pure ethics of consumerism will not be enough!

Mark Kaufmann published an interesting analysis of the advertising measures of the oil company British Petroleum (BP) on mashable.com.[16] BP had, on its website, provided a calculator that allowed invidiual consumers to calculate their carbon footprint. Kaufmann proves that BP was trying to distract from its own culpability by assigning the blame for the use of fossil energy sources to individuals and, at the same time, suggested that state measures were not necessary. This does not, however, mean that consumers, as citizens, do not have their share of responsibility. It might be true that consumers can only choose among goods that are being offered to them, and are therefore only able to set new trends very slowly. Often they also have to spend more money if they adopt a trail blazing role in certain areas. Such commitment is commanded by ethics and deserves high respect, but it will be impossible to turn the tide soley by changing the patterns of consumptions. It is, rather, necessary that the state, or, even better, the states, internationally coordinated, pursue an economic policy which punishes an ecologically problematic use of raw materials through duties and taxes, but, at the same time, creates a framework for the development of alternatives by economic incentives, clear and reliable decisions and the support of releveant research. For this, of course, the political commitment of citizens who are aware of global connections is necessary, and who become involved even if the problems seem to be far removed at first glance (or far in the future). The pressure from below is necessary, like, for example, modelled by the 'Fridays for future' movement, or by how it is pursued by non governmental organisations in the area of mining, in Germany, for example, by the campaign 'Pit Peru: wealth leaves, poverty stays.' [17]

Translated by Katharina Smith-Mueller

Notes

1. For a good general overview cf. Florian Neukirchen/Gunnar Ries, Die Welt der Rohstoffe. Lagerstätten, Förderung und wirtschaftliche Aspekte, Berlin/Heidelberg 2016 .
2. Cf. Christophe McGlade/Paul Ekins, The geographical distribution of fossil fuels unused when limiting global warming to 2 °C, in: Nature 517/7533 (2015), 187–190.
3. The term probably comes from W. Max Corden, Booming Sector and Dutch Disease Economics. Survey and Consolidation, in: Oxford Economic Papers 36 (1984), 359–380.

4. Cf. Jeffrey D. Sachs/Andrew M. Warner, Natural Resource Abundance and Economic Growth, in: National Bureau of Economic Research Working Paper Series 5398 (1995).
5. Cf. Michael L. Ross, What Have We Learned about the Resource Curse?, in: Annual Review of Political Science 18/1 (2015), 239–259.
6. Cf. Thomas Pogge, Weltarmut und Menschenrechte. Kosmopolitische Verantwortung und Reformen, Frankfurt am Main/New York 2011, 205—210.
7. For Latin America, cf. e.g. Juan Cruz Vieyra/Malaika Masson, Transparent governance in an age of abundance. Experiences from the extractive industries in Latin America and the Caribbean, Washington D.C. 2014.
8. On the following cf. In total our analysis on neo-extractivism in Bolivia: Gerhard Kruip/Dietmar Müßig/Raphael Zikesch (ed.), Neo-Extraktivismus in Bolivien. Chancen, Risiken, Nachhaltigkeit, Münster 2019. – Spanish edition: El Neo-Extractivismo en Bolivia. Oportunidades, Riesgos, Sostenibilidad, Cochabamba (Bolivien) 2019. Useful and recent information can also be found on the website of the Fundación Jubiléo: https://jubileobolivia.org.bo.
9. Eduardo Gudynas, Neo-Extraktivismus und Ausgleichsmechanismen der progressiven südamerikanischen Regierungen, in: Kurswechsel 3 (2011), 72; cf. id., Value, Growth, Development. South American Lessons for a New Ecopolitics, in: Capitalism Nature Socialism 30/2 (2019), 234–243.
10. Cf. Raphael Hierzu Zikesch, Die Generierung und Entwicklung der staatlichen Ölrente Boliviens zwischen 2006 und 2016, in: Kruip/Müßig/Zikesch (ed.), Neo-Extraktivismus in Bolivien, 99–108 and, for the most recent data of the coutnry profile of Bolivia by the Federal Statistical Office https://www.destatis.de/DE/Themen/Laender-Regionen/Internationales/Laenderprofile/bolivien.pdf?__blob=publicationFile.
11. Accordig to data from the World Bank https://www.macrotrends.net/countries/BOL/bolivia/poverty-rate.
12. I generalise, and I am summarising our final recommendations, cf. Kruip/Müßig/Zikesch, Empfehlungen, in: id. (ed.), Neo-Extraktivismus in Bolivien, 325—330..
13. Cf. on this Gerhard Kruip, Umweltethik und Nachhaltigkeit in christlicher Perspektive, in: Ralph Bergold/Jochen Sautermeister/André Schröder (ed.), Dem Wandel eine menschliche Gestalt geben. Sozialethische Perspektiven für die Gesellschaft von morgen, Freiburg et al. 2017, 319—332.
14. Cf. Gudynas, Value, Growth, Development.
15. As a classic on this cf. Michel Albert, Capitalisme contre capitalisme, Paris 1991.
16. Cf. Mark Kaufmann, The carbon footprint sham. A 'successful, deceptive' PR campaign, available online under: https://mashable.com/feature/carbon-footprint-pr-campaign-sham/?europe=true.
17. See their website on http://www.kampagne-bergwerk-peru.de/.

Part Two: Analysis of the Issue

The Politics of Forest Conservation: Ethical Dilemmas and Impact on Peacebuilding

Léocadie Lushombo, Ph.D.

Reducing Emissions from Deforestation and Forest Degradation (REDD+) aims to contribute to climate change mitigation efforts. However, REDD+'s vision is riddled with ethical dilemmas due to its technological and market-based instruments. The policy at work regarding forests conservation in the Congo Basin is a one-fits-for-all to climate change mitigation, that, by treating conservation as a monetary issue, constitutes a threat to peacebuilding. This paper concludes that participation of local communities and relationships of trust in the management of the tropical forests are a crucial means of sustainable conservation and are a peacebuilding tool. The Congo Basin vindicates Pope Francis' claim that real peace is possible only where independence and responsibility are shared.

The Congo Basin covers six countries in Central Africa, including Cameroon, Central African Republic (CAR), The Republic of Congo, The Democratic Republic of Congo (DRC), Equatorial Guinea, and Gabon. It is the second largest forest in the world, following the Amazon and covers approximately 530 million hectares of land, with 300 million hectares of forest.[1] According to environmental scientists, besides the Congo Basin's carbon sequestration and storing potential that constitutes a priceless treasure for the global greenhouse emissions balance, approximately 60 million people living inside or in their vicinity, and urban centers are dependent on the forests for their livelihoods, social, and cultural life.[2]

Considering the potential of the Congo Basin rainforest, this paper claims that better politics of management and conservation of forests are, in fact, a form of peacebuilding. Any mismanagement of the Congo Basin forests is a threat to peace in Central Africa, a threat to its economic development and political stability. Considering that the DRC is the largest country of the Congo Basin, with the largest population and largest rainforest, which is estimated to 167 million hectares[3]; this paper focuses on DRC forests and policy management, particularly policy related to conservation of forests under the United Nations mechanism *Réduction des Émissions dues à la Déforestation et à la Dégradation* (REDD+). The DRC is "home to one of the world's most advanced jurisdictional REDD+"[4] programs and one of the first countries in Central Africa to obtain validation of its 2010–2012 preparedness plan REDD+.[5]

REDD+ is a "form of payment for ecosystem services (PES) schemes" to ensure carbon sequestration – a process of capturing and storing atmospheric carbon dioxide to reduce the amount of carbon dioxide in the atmosphere to reduce global warming.[6] REDD+ also aims to advance sustainable development in tropical forest countries. Hundreds of millions of dollars are poured into REDD+ project to conserve forests but little is being said on the ethical dilemmas, social impacts, and peace disturbance of such a project.

DRC's millions of forested areas are recognized as reservoirs of greenhouse gases.[7] The DRC's carbon sinks can hold "27,258 million tons of carbon,"[8] crucial to face the threat of global warming and critical to function as "global ecosystem service provider."[9] Though the proportion of current rate of deforestation of the DRC's and the Congo Basin as a whole is considered relatively low, it is estimated that by 2050, deforestation will climb.

Pays	Total land area (1000 ha)	Population			Forest Land (1000 ha)	% of Land	Deforestation rate(%)	
		2006	2025	2050			1990-2000	2000-2005
Cameroon	46,540	17.3	24	32.3	21,245	45.6	0.9	1.0
Central Africa	62,298	4.3	5.5	6.5	22,755	36.5	0.1	0.1
Congo	34,150	3.7	5.9	9.7	22,471	65.8	0.1	0.1
DR Congo	226,705	62.7	108.0	183.2	133,610	58.9	0.4	0.2
Equatorial Guinea	2805	0.5	0.8	1.1	1,632	58.2	0.6	0.9
Gabon	25,767	1.4	1.8	2.3	21,775	84.5	ns	ns

Illustration: General Information on countries in Central Africa[10]

This climbing of deforestation suggests the need of sustainable forest conservation politics.

This paper argues that the policy at work regarding forest conservation in the Congo Basin – a one-fits-for-all approach to climate change mitigation that treats conservation as a monetary issue – can more likely undermine peacebuilding. This paper draws on community forestry's vision and experience that allows full participation of local communities as a peacebuilding tool. REDD+, like all other funds involved in forest conservation, are examples of dynamics of power that can undermine peace. Peace is sowed when we walk alongside the excluded, the abandoned, and the powerless (*Fratelli Tutti* (FT), 2) Money alone cannot address deforestation in areas where local communities are likely evicted from lands for conservation purposes. Favoring conservation or preservation of forests while overlooking the need of local communities for food crops, hunting or fishing is an inherent source of conflicts.

I. Social Impacts of Deforestation and Degradation of the Congo Basin Forests

The first factor that explains the deforestation in the DRC is the influx of 2 million refugees from neighboring countries that increased since the Rwandese genocide in April 1994.[11] The influx of refugees was followed by the invasion of the DRC by Ugandan and Rwandan foreign forces and the irruption of other armed groups that included militias from the DRC itself.[12] Human Rights records documented that armed groups not only confiscated lands, but also cut trees down, and "forced civilians to cut and transport wood and to dig in mines on [their] behalf."[13] These realities have a negative impact on forest canopy.

The second factor is the international business in the Congo Basin. The summary of traceable exports by-product in the province of North Kivu (DRC) for 2012 that had been published by *Commission Episcopale pour la Gestion des Ressources Naturelles* (CERN) indicates that millions of kilograms of cassiterite and thousands of kilograms of coltan have been exported to China and Hong-Kong, for the year 2012. As for gold, a significant quantity has been exported to The United Arab Emirates. It is important to note that even with mining, forests and biodiversity suffer a setback.

CERN has recently done other work too, selecting 101 artisanal mining sites in the same Northern Province of the DRC. The study showed that of the hundred mining sites listed, almost 86.4% are located in concessions that include forests or other biodiversity. Whether legal or illegal, these mining products are often sold outside the DRC through the neighboring countries, threatening the integrity of the forest ecosystem, and producing no sustainable return for the peoples.[14]

China's logging trade activities are impacting African Forests in considerable ways. According to Quartz Africa, Chinese investment in Africa is growing faster, and its trend is not taking sustainable paths for the African peoples. The International Institute for Environment and Development (IIED) reports that around 75% of African timber exports are sent to China, making China "the largest importer and processor" of African logs. Besides purchasing timber from local concessions, Chinese operators, like any other logger, can acquire forests as allowed by the DRC's Forest Law. Millions of hectares are delivered to loggers for 25 or 50 years and perpetual use. Several national bans have restricted unprocessed logs in Africa, but these bans are ineffective because non-enforced.[15]

A third factor explaining the deforestation and degradation of the DRC forests is its demographic explosion that is expected to almost a triple by 2050 as shown in the figure above.[16] All the above factors are the "signs that things are now reaching a breaking point." (*Laudato Sí* (LS), 61) There is no doubt that the forests of the Congo Basin need to be conserved to mitigate global warming. The Kyoto Protocol and the Paris Agreement are of good purpose.

The Paris Agreement, signed in December 2015, promoted compensation of actors for reducing forest-related carbon emissions through public REDD+ finance in the international effort to combat climate change by reducing carbon dioxide emissions.[17] The DRC signed the latter Agreement in April 2016 and ratified it in December 2017, committing to work to ensure its *Contribution Déterminée à l'échelle Nationale* (CDN) – a DRC's commitment to reduce 17% of its GHG emissions at a national scale between 2020 and 2030. However, this agreement does suggest many controversies and ethical dilemmas that endanger peacebuilding in the region.

II. Conservation of the Congo Basin, Ethical Dilemmas, and Concerns for Peace

Pope Francis suggests that aspiration to "a world that provides land, housing and works for all" is "the true path of peace." Real peace will be possible only where independence and responsibility are shared. (FT, 127) The path to peace is about "getting people to work together, side-by-side, in pursuing goals that benefit everyone." (FT, 228) For the sake of peace, I take issue with REDD+ or any other funding trends that "hinder the development of universal fraternity" (FT, 9) by reinforcing economic dependance of the tropical forests' regions toward developed countries rather than solidarizing with the local peoples, for them to take their responsibilities for sustainability.

REDD+ does promote a legitimate goal of conservation, however, it is missing the "working together, side-by-side" – a shared responsibility and benefits. It is missing participation of the people that I argue is pillar of peacebuilding. The politics of conservation of REDD+ are cautionary example of what Pope Francis calls the danger of focusing on technical solutions imported from developed countries leaving behind local cultures that can help to build harmony and peace in the tropical forests' regions (LS, 144, 200).

Pope Francis, in his call to protect tropical forests, he encourages conservation of forests to help mitigate climate change. (LS, 24) However, he stands against "proposals to internationalize the Amazon, which only serve the economic interests of transnational corporations." (LS, 38)

He warns about a leadership and a "new power structures based on the techno-economic paradigm" that "may overwhelm not only our politics but also freedom and justice" (LS, 53) and hinders the development of universal fraternity. (FT, 9) Development takes into account local cultures and requires involvement of the peoples. Imposing a vision of development that is pushed into local peoples and cultures can have disastrous consequences as do deforestation and degradation. (LS, 145) Too many interests do manipulate, not only information but the protection of biodiversity and plans to mitigate climate change (LS, 54) obstructing the common good and leading to violence. (LS, 157)

Cecilia Luttrell, Kate Schreckenberg, and Leo Peskett argue that the REDD+'s protocols for conservation do reinforce the market-based instrument with a focus on carbon financing whose primary aim "is to offset emissions and not to bring about pro-poor development."[18] Forests conservation, though relevant to mitigation, imperils peace. I understand peace as "not the absence of violence, but tranquility, concord, a set of properly ordered relations within or between human beings."[19] Peacebuilders thrive to create social order that ensures participation of all in such a way that no voice should be ignored or dismissed. Political authority has responsibility to consider the people's wisdom, especially in the communities where there are already conflicts and tensions due to unjust distribution of the goods. In this perspective, proponents of peacebuilding are "convinced that dignity, rights, and human security are best served by replacing cycles of violence with relations of trust"[20] and challenge structural injustice and mechanisms that fuel conflicts.

Peacebuilding goes beyond the "win-win-win"[21] politics of conservation to ensure that local communities share from the benefits of the forests upon which depends their livelihood. Peacebuilding is also fostered through a cohesive and inclusive policy that encourages local participation toward making a positive sum of their capabilities rather than repeating the colonial framework. Peacebuilding is about investing in understanding the power unbalance that leads to conflicts rather than focusing only on technical solutions already set up by industrialized countries and that, as pope Francis suggests, ensure the interests of the powerful. These solutions, by their extravert character, do not empower local communities and lead to dependance at all levels.

The Jesuit Rigobert Minani corroborates the importance of considering local wisdom when he argues that one of the plausible explanations why the UN struggles to bring peace in the DRC despite its huge effort and apparent goodwill is "the failure of the various peace efforts to consult, much less involved effectively, local communities, and leaders."[22] The non-involvement of local communities or non-recognition of their traditional wisdom can be source of conflicts – "the marketplace, by itself, cannot resolve every problem." (FT, 168)

Théophile Gata, one responsible for a local NGO that works for conservation with indigenous peoples for decades, suggests that most of the conflicts are born from land use and ownership. There are conflicts between loggers themselves, between loggers and the local communities, between the latter and the state; and between the local loggers and the industrial private loggers to whom the DRC's legal system concedes lands.[23] The relations between these groups seem to be infected by a race for money dedicated to conservation of forests. The mistrust that is being instituted around money, according a survey Collectif de Défenseurs de l'Environnement (CODE) conducted in 2018 on 10 years of REDD+, has incalculable consequences for local communities.

According to Milburn, REDD+ provides to the DRC "the potential to earn US$1 billion from carbon markets," through the Ibi Batéké carbon sink plantation (IBCSP) project alone.[24] This is a Mai Ndombe REDD+ project (a Central West province of the DRC), where many conflicts related to forest management have been already noted. This project exceeds $90 million for an area of 12.3 million hectares representing 123,000 km2 (approximatively the size of the entire England), of which there are 9.8 million hectares of forests.[25] But the bigger is the money invested the more conflicts are fueled.

Pope Francis rightly denounces this monetary-oriented approach when he warns us not to overlook how global economic interests "can undermine individual nations' sovereignty under the guise of protecting [the forests]" and how the internalization of the Amazon can serve the economic interests of transnational corporations. (LS, 38) Forest conservation in the Congo Basin is a long-standing political issue in international negotiations that involve several international interests that can be seen through the many partners involved in conservation programs investing millions of dollars in forestry projects.[26] There is no doubt that these programs are not without particular interests nor will they be done without conflict. The idea of compensating an actor for reducing forest-related carbon emissions through public REDD+ finance "serves to disperse and displace, rather than resolve, policy-making on non-carbon values."[27] Funding carbon stock sequestration can undermine the local communities' rights and so fragilize peacebuilding.

A network of 13 civil society observers for the Basin Congo from Mai-Ndombe and the neighboring provinces of Equateur (North-west DRC province) suggests that conflicts arise from the failure of the program REDD+ to obtain "the free, prior and informed consent of local communities," the promise of benefices that are still not delivered to local communities, the lack of proper representation of local communities into the project, the "insufficient effort to clarify and strengthen the tenure security of local communities, leaving them vulnerable to land speculation and migration," the inadequate "representation of the traditional land use systems" of local communities that have caused disputes between them over lands boundaries, cut off women's livelihoods and local communities' access to food. This scarcity of food due to conservation of forests led a community to burn savannahs they were untrusted to protect because they had not received payment expected. REDD+ has also limited local governments' capacity in its jurisdictional program.[28]

The interests make it possible for these big and multi-funds programs to leave behind a crucial problem like that of overpopulation in Mai-Ndombe. The devastating factors on the overpopulated communities have been called upon by *Réseau Ecclésial du Bassin du Congo* (REBAC).[29] Bishop Bafuidinsoni explains that acquiring large and several logging concessions either for timber exploitation or for conservation is becoming harmful to the local communities rather than increasing their potential for productivity, particularly because of the demographic pressure and the increased need to access lands[30] and benefit from carbon-storing.

Bishop Bafuidinsoni also noted the case of numerous conflicts linked to the non-equitable distribution of income from natural resources in the Mai-Ndombe region that the DRC has been helplessly observing since the colonial period. This plunder of natural resources is without fair compensation and is accompanied by evictions. As Pope Francis recalls, "[e]conomies of scale, especially in the agricultural sector, end up forcing smallholders to sell their land or to abandon their traditional crops." (LS, 129) These injustices are, first of all, governmental responsibility. Though legalized, they undermine peace in so far as, "the advance of this kind of globalism strengthens the identity of the more powerful, who can protect themselves, but it tends to diminish the identity of the weaker and poorer regions, making them more vulnerable and dependent." (FT, 12)

Rendering the local communities vulnerable and dependent (even when this negative outcome is not intended) poisons peacebuilding – the "market forces may be more destructive than military forces." [31] The ability of markets to fuel conflicts that already exist and create new ones seems to be overlooked by carbon markets.

The UN's engagement approach in the DRC peace efforts tends to apply a generic model of actions to be taken to build peace, and it is a "one-size-fits-all approach [that] does not work in all cases and has repeatedly failed."[32] This approach seems to be the dominant one in the conservation endorsed by REDD+. Little or no attention is paid to the land tenure insecurity of local communities; land grabbing and the price inflation; customary practices and sharecropping; and the risks of conflicts due to the displacement of populations and capture of REDD+ benefits by some and not by other groups or communities. Besides, the role of women in land management and initiative-taking remains marginalized.[33]

Pope Francis suggests that "everything is interconnected, and that genuine care for our own lives and our relationships with nature is inseparable from fraternity, justice, and faithfulness to others." (LS, 70) Community forestry provides hope toward a relationship with nature that preserves fraternity, justice, a relation of trust, and consequently peace.

III. Community Forestry Could Be an Efficacious Peacebuilding Machine

Community forestry that regroups the Indigenous Peoples and Local Communities (IPLC) can serve as peacebuilder through deforestation, degradation, and sustainable conservation.

Article 22 of the DRC's 2002 Forest Code grants to local communities, part of the total area of forest concessions that are managed under customary laws. Any IPLC can obtain a forest concession existing in its area but not exceeding 50,000 ha. This grant is free of charge. This practice is more sustainable and constitutes a hope for the future as a means to render local communities responsible for conservation while ensuring sustainable economic subsistence.

Community forestry (CFCL)[34] promotes peace mainly through its participatory processes. It brings diverse cultural differences together and allows access to land endowed with a legal status. Community forestry empowers the IPLC to negotiate with the local government the right to usufruct before being victims of any eviction.[35] A community can access legal status only through the IPLC structure.

The legal status of the IPLC also decreases conflicts between communities and industrial loggers who have often been conceded larger areas of forests, including areas that the IPLC consider theirs by customary law. Once the IPLC are legally granted lands, they are habilitated to subcontracting with industrial loggers. In this way, they continue to look after their people's well-being, making sure benefits are fairly shared, conflicts between loggers and local communities are settled, and trust is built up.

Women are the first economic agents in local areas and have been excluded from decision-making processes for a long time. The Green Belt Movement (GBM), founded by Wangari Maathai in Kenya in 1977, has been a source of inspiration in including women. This movement has put to light and confirmed that climate resilience requires democratic spaces at the grassroots levels and must not be separated from fraternity and sisterhood. The GBM movement has also shown that women already responsible for the family's livelihood are pillars to this resilience. Politics of conservation that leave behind these women are undermining cohesion and economic power at the family and social levels.

Pope Francis suggests that it is essential "to avoid the 'temptation to appeal to the law of force rather than to the force of law'." (FT, 174) Community forestry provides means to resist appealing to the law of force when faced with injustices, evictions, and unfair distribution of the goods of forests. Community forestry constitutes what pope Francis suggests as "normative instruments for the peaceful resolution of controversies." (FT, 174) It is a means through which the powerful can be reminded that our common home belongs to the powerless as well. It provides space where different groups can discuss partisan interests to promote peaceful coexistence. (FT, 232)

Community forestry provides spaces where a little flame deep in local communities' hearts can "be extinguished before it turns into a great blaze," (FT, 243) a means where fraternity can take shape and a chance is given to everyone to be involved in the shaping paths to peace, especially in the context of conflicts.

Notes

1. Carole Megevand/Aline Mosnier, Deforestation Trends in the Congo Basin: Reconciling Economic Growth and Forest Protection, Washington D.C.: World Bank, 2013, 1.
2. Carlos de Wasseige/Martin Tadoum/Richard Eba 'a Atyi/Charles Doumenge (eds.), The Forests of the Congo Basin: Forests and Climate Change, Neufchâteau: Weyrich Edition, 2015, 17.
3. Megevand/Mosnier, Deforestation Trends, 13.
4. Norah Berk/Prince Lungungu, "REDD-Minus: The Rhetoric and Reality of the Mai Ndombe REDD+ Programme," RainForest Foundation UK, December 2020, 1, at https://www.rainforestfoundationuk.org/media.ashx/redd-minus.pdf.
5. Collectif de Défenseurs de l'Environnement (CODE), "Sondage Sur Les Dix Ans Du Processus REDD+ En République Démocratique Du Congo: Synthèse Des Résultats/ Sondage Mené Du 05 Au 20 Octobre 2018," 4.
6. Richard Milburn, "The Roots to Peace in the Democratic Republic of Congo: Conservation as a Platform for Green Development," International Affairs 90.4 (2014), 871–887, here 880, https://doi.org/10.1111/1468-2346.12145.
7. Megevand/Mosnier, Deforestation Trends, 33.
8. Milburn, "The Roots to Peace in the Democratic Republic of Congo," 877.
9. UNEP (United Nations Environment Programme), The Democratic Republic of the Congo: Post-Conflict Environmental Assessment: Synthesis for Policy Makers, Nairobi, 2011, 22.
10. Mekou Youssoufa Bele/Denis Jean Sonwa/Anne-Marie Tiani, "Adapting the Congo Basin forests management to climate change: Linkages among biodiversity, forest loss, and human well-being," Forest Policy and Economics, 50 (2015), 1□10, here 4, https://doi.org/10.1016/j.forpol.2014.05.010.
11. Rigobert Minani Bihuzo, "Building Peace in the Democratic Republic of the Congo: Beyond the United Nations Toolkit," The Southern Voices Network for Peacebuliding 26 (2020), 1□7.
12. United Nations Security Council, "Unanimously Adopting Resolution 1332 (2000), Extends Democratic Republic of Congo Mission Until 15 June," 14 December 2000, at https://www.un.org/press/en/2000/sc6975.doc.htm.
13. United Nations Security Council, "Letter dated 12 November 2012 from the Chair of the Security Council Committee established pursuant to resolution 1533 (2004) concerning the Democratic Republic of the Congo addressed to the President of the Security Council," S/2012/843, 15 November 2012, at http://digitallibrary.un.org/record/738098.

14. Bele/Sonwa/Tiani, "Adapting the Congo Basin Forests Management to Climate Change," 5.
15. Bo Li, "Five Ways China's Overseas Investments Are Impacting African Forests," Quartz Africa, 10 February 2016, at https://qz.com/africa/613965/.
16. United Nations Department of Economic and Social Affairs, "World Population Prospects 2019, Online Edition. Rev. 1.," at https://population.un.org/wpp/Download/Standard/Population/ [05 November 2020].
17. Marleen Buizer/David Humphreys/Will de Jong, "Climate change and deforestation: The evolution of an intersecting policy domain," Environmental Science & Policy 35 (2014), 1□11, here 4, https://doi.org/10.1016/j.envsci.2013.06.001.
18. Cecilia Luttrell/Kate Schreckenberg/Leo Peskett, "The Implications of Carbon Financing for Pro-Poor Community Forestry," Forest Policy and Environment Programme (fpep), Forestry Briefing 14 (2007), 2, at https://www.odi.org/sites/odi.org.uk/files/odi-assets/publications-opinion-files/610.pdf.
19. Richard Brian Miller, Interpretations of Conflict: Ethics, Pacifism, and the Just-War Tradition, Chicago: University of Chicago Press, 1991, 21.
20. Lisa Sowle Cahill, Blessed Are the Peacemakers: Pacifism, Just War, and Peacebuilding, Minneapolis: Fortress Press, 2019, 5–6.
21. Buizer/ Humphreys/de Jong, "Climate change and deforestation,“ 7.
22. Minani Bihuzo, "Building Peace in the Democratic Republic of the Congo,“ 3.
23. Théophile Gata Dikulukila, "Typologie Des Conflits Liés à l'exploitation Industrielle Du Bois Dans La Province Du Kongo Central (RDC)," in Concessions à La Pauvreté: Les Impacts Environnementaux, Sociaux et Économiques Des Concessions d'exploitation Forestière Industrielles Sur Les Forêts Tropicales Africaines (RainForest Foundation/Forests Monitor, 2007), 47–48.
24. Milburn, "The Roots to Peace in the Democratic Republic of Congo,“ 880.
25. Marine Gauthier, "Mai-Ndombe: le laboratoire de la REDD+ bénéficiera-t-il aux Peuples Autochtones et communautés locales? https://rightsandresources.org/fr/publication/mai-ndombe-le-laboratoire-de-la-redd-beneficiera-t-il-aux-peuples-autochtones-et-communautes-locales/.
26. Food and Agriculture Organization of the United Nations (FAO), "REDD+ initiatives," at http://www.fao.org/redd/initiatives/en.
27. Buizer/ Humphreys/de Jong, "Climate change and deforestation,“ 1.
28. Berk/Lungungu, "REDD-Minus,“ 1–8.
29 Church Network for the Congo Basin.
30. Global Catholic Climate Movement, "Amazonian Network Dear to Pope Francis Now Has a Sister Organization in the Congo Rainforest," accessed February 13, 2021, https://catholicclimatemovement.global/amazonian-network-dear-to-pope-francis-now-has-a-sister-organization-in-the-congo-rainforest/.
31 Jeffrey A. McNeely, "Overview A: Biodiversity, Conflict and Tropical Forests," in Richard Matthew/Mark Halle/Jason Switzer (eds.), Conserving the Peace: Resources, Livelihoods and Security, Winnipeg: International Institute for Sustainable Development, 2002, 29–56, here 45.
32. Minani Bihuzo, "Building Peace in the Democratic Republic of the Congo,“ 4.
33. Gauthier, "Mai-Ndombe,“ 10-11.
34. English expression of "concession forestcrie des communautés locales (CFCL)."
35. Théophile Gata Dikulukila, "Community Forestry in the DRC: Heading in the Right Direction but Challenges Lay Ahead," Forest Echoes 2 (2014), 7.

Amazonia Gift: to Right the Wrongs

Fr. Cedric Prakash SJ

'Amazonia Gift: to Right the Wrongs' focuses on Pope Francis' Apostolic Exhortation 'Querida Amazonia' *and its global relevance. The exhortation needs to be seen as a challenge to address the human rights violations that are heaped on the indigenous peoples, the poor and other vulnerable sections and on the environment. The 1986 period film* The Mission *serves as an apt backgrounder to the realities of today and to possible responses. A way forward is also finally proposed to ensure that directions from Church do not stay in the realm of words and ideas, but are put into practice.*

The Mission[1] is a 1986 British period drama film about the experiences of a Jesuit missionary in 18th-century South America. The film is a rather complex one though compelling and spiritually stirring. In essence, it is about the stand which the Spanish Jesuits take to protect the identity of a remote South American tribe (the Guarani Indian people – an indigenous people of the Amazon). The film is intertwined in the political pressures of a colonial power, the predatory racism of European settlers who are basically pro-slavery and the pragmatic needs of the Jesuit order (and Church) of that time.

The Mission is based on historical facts surrounding the 1750 Treaty of Madrid in which Spain ceded part of its territories in Paraguay to Portugal, mainly the areas where the Jesuits had their missions. The interesting aspect of this movie is that there is an important subtext: the impending suppression of the Society of Jesus in most parts of Western Europe (beginning in 1759, formalised in 1773 and which ended only in 1814). The film portrays the resilience of the Guarani people despite all odds and the efforts of the Jesuits to accompany them (though there is a clear divergence in strategy of the two Jesuit protagonists in the film) in order to protect their rights, their customs and above all from being swallowed in the lucrative slave-market of that time.

The film deals with bureaucratic hassles, political and religious machinations, intrigue, greed for power and profits among other human frailties; however, at the same time it also focuses on the challenges and hostilities that one must face when one attempts to take on the system, the powers (vested interests). Above all, it is a film about "mission", what it entails when disciples of Jesus actually demonstrate that unflinching courage to go forth to the peripheries.

More than thirty-four years after it was first released (and won international acclaim and awards), the film is ranked today as number one on the Church Times' Top 50 Religious Films list and features as one of the fifteen films in the 'religious' category of the Vatican Film list. *The Mission Carries a Message from Past to Present* was a very significant title given by Judith Miller in a very detailed review in the New York Times.[2] Certainly, *The Mission* is an apt backgrounder to the post-synodal Apostolic Exhortation of Pope Francis *Querida Amazonia*[3] and of the need and importance of addressing and acting on the wrongs inflicted on the people of God and on the common home which He has entrusted to our care.

I. *Querida Amazonia*

Pope Francis addresses *Querida Amazonia*, "To the People of God and to All Persons of Good Will", saying:

> I am addressing the present Exhortation to the whole world. I am doing so to help awaken their affection and concern for that land which is also 'ours', and to invite them to value it and acknowledge it as a sacred mystery. But also, because the Church's concern for the problems of this area obliges us to discuss, however briefly, a number of other important issues that can assist other areas of our world in confronting their own challenges. (#5)

He then shares his four dreams:

> I dream of an Amazon region that fights for the rights of the poor, the original peoples and the least of our brothers and sisters, where their voices can be heard and their dignity advanced.
> I dream of an Amazon region that can preserve its distinctive cultural riches, where the beauty of our humanity shines forth in so many varied ways.
> I dream of an Amazon region that can jealously preserve its overwhelming natural beauty and the superabundant life teeming in its rivers and forests.
> I dream of Christian communities capable of generous commitment, incarnate in the Amazon region, and giving the Church new faces with Amazonian features. (#7)

The dreams are inter-related; one cannot be separated from the other. In *Querida Amazonia*, Pope Francis weaves them into a tapestry of social, cultural, ecological, and ecclesial threads deep in theology; however, his opening remarks in his social dream sets the tone for what follows:

> Our dream is that of an Amazon region that can integrate and promote all its inhabitants, enabling them to enjoy 'good living'. But this calls for a prophetic plea and an arduous effort on behalf of the poor. For though it is true that the Amazon region is facing an ecological disaster, it also has to be made clear that 'a true ecological approach' always becomes a social approach; it must integrate questions of justice in debates on the environment, so as to hear both the cry of the earth and the cry of the poor. We do not need an environmentalism that is concerned for the biome but ignores the Amazonian peoples. (#8)

These words also resonate with his 'no-holds-barred' Encyclical letter, *Laudato Si*[4] (On Care for our Common Home) which on May 24, 2015, the Solemnity of Pentecost, he addressed "to every person living on the planet." On May 24, 2020, the fifth anniversary of this path-breaking and incisive Encyclical, Pope Francis said that the document sought to, "call attention to the cry of the Earth and of the poor." He invited everyone to take part in the *Laudato Si* Year from 24 May 2020 until 24 May 2021 saying, "I invite all people of goodwill to take part, to care for our common home and our most vulnerable brothers and sisters."

II. A Gift to Right the Wrongs

Querida Amazonia must necessarily be seen as a gift to right the wrongs; a challenge to address the human rights violations that are heaped on the indigenous peoples, the poor and the other vulnerable and also on the earth. These include climate change, global warming, the rapacious destruction of natural resources, a neo-colonialism portrayed in xenophobia and exclusiveness, migration, the growing gap between the rich and poor, the denial of rights and freedoms (particularly to indigenous peoples and minorities), exclusiveness and divisiveness, violence, the emergence of majoritarian and dictatorial regimes. We witness this and experience this happening all over the world particularly in continents and nations in the Southern Hemisphere; whilst *Querida Amazonia* has its focus in the nations in and around the Amazon basin, the realities and the human rights violations that grip that area are the same ones that grip peoples and nations across the globe. One however needs truth and non-violence to address these grim realities.

Mahatma Gandhi puts it poignantly in his powerful autobiography, *The Story of My Experiments with Truth*[5]:

> But this much I can say with assurance, as a result of all my experiments, that a perfect vision of Truth can only follow a complete realization of Ahimsa. To see the universal and all-pervading Spirit of Truth face to face one must be able to love the meanest of creation as oneself. And a man who aspires after that cannot afford to keep out of any field of life.

For him truth and ahimsa (non-violence) complement each other and are essential in any attempt to right the wrongs. Meaningful engagement in the lives of others is only possible when these two are in place.

II.i The Rights of the Indigenous Peoples

Indigenous peoples are the most affected everywhere. In India, according to the 2011 Census (the last official Census in the country), there are more than 104 million (approx. 8.6% of the population) indigenous peoples (also known in India as Adivasis or tribals) making it the largest tribal population in the world. The States which have large tribal populations are Madhya Pradesh, Chhattisgarh, Orissa, Gujarat, Jharkhand, Rajasthan, Lakshadweep, and the North Eastern States. Adivasis or tribals have their own distinct cultures, customs, languages and even religion. For centuries, Adivasis have been living in the sylvan and secure environment of the forest. However, over the years, they have been subjected to exploitation and injustices. In the name of 'development', they have been gradually alienated from the natural resources to which they have a claim from time immemorial.

The fact remains that a fairly large percentage of the country's natural resources are in the areas populated by India's indigenous peoples. Lopsided development programmes and the wanton destruction of the forests and the eco-systems by rapacious mining companies and other mega-projects have meant the displacement of hundreds and thousands of tribals over the years.

Pope Francis in *Laudato S*i emphasises this dimension,

> It is essential to show special care for indigenous communities and their cultural traditions. They are not merely one minority among others, but should be the principal dialogue partners, especially when large projects affecting their land are proposed. For them, land is not a commodity but rather a gift from God and from their ancestors who rest there, a sacred space with which they need to interact if they are to maintain their identity and values. When they remain on their land, they themselves care for it best. Nevertheless, in various parts of the world, pressure is being put on them to abandon their homelands to make room for agricultural or mining projects which are undertaken without regard for the degradation of nature and culture. (#146)

In 1996, as a response to the growing Adivasi struggles in many parts (particularly the Eastern belt), the Government introduced the Panchayats Extension to Scheduled Areas Act (PESA) and later in 2006 the Forests Rights Act (FRA). Both PESA and FRA were introduced with the intention of undoing the centuries of historical injustice wrought on the Adivasis;

however, while granting community rights over their lands and forests, both these Acts have denied the tribals the ownership of natural resources. Like indigenous peoples in many parts of the world, the Adivasis are gradually being evicted from the areas which they once called their home.

Several Adivasis have also begun their struggle against the State. Their argument is that if the Government of the day sides only with the corporate sector and other vested interests, in denying them what is rightfully theirs, they have no choice but to protest! Fr Stan Swamy is a Jesuit priest who has been accompanying the Adivasis in their quest for justice and for a more dignified life. On 8 October 2020, this eighty-three-year-old priest was arrested from his residence in Ranchi, Jharkhand on fabricated charges and today is incarcerated in the Taloja Prison near Mumbai. Taking a visible and vocal stand for the rights of indigenous peoples necessarily comes with a price as the film, The Mission so powerfully portrays.

II.ii. The Rights of the Poor

In an attempt to reach out to the poor and to help alleviate their conditions, Pope Francis introduced the 'World Day of the Poor', four years ago, which is observed on the Sunday before the Feast of Christ the King. Pope Francis' message for this year's World Day of the Poor (15 November 2020)[6] was based on the theme, Stretch forth your hand to the poor. He says:

> At the same time, the command: 'Stretch forth your hand to the poor', challenges the attitude of those who prefer to keep their hands in their pockets and to remain unmoved by situations of poverty in which they are often complicit. Indifference and cynicism are their daily food. What a difference from the generous hands we have described! If they stretch out their hands, it is to touch computer keys to transfer sums of money from one part of the world to another, ensuring the wealth of an elite few and the dire poverty of millions and the ruin of entire nations. Some hands are outstretched to accumulate money by the sale of weapons that others, including those of children, use to sow death and poverty. Other hands are outstretched to deal doses of death in dark alleys in order to grow rich and live in luxury and excess, or to quietly pass a bribe for the sake of quick and corrupt gain. Others still,

> parading a sham respectability, lay down laws which they themselves do not observe...... Almost without being aware of it, we end up being incapable of feeling compassion at the outcry of the poor, weeping for other people's pain, and feeling a need to help them, as though all this were someone else's responsibility and not our own.

There is a paradigm shift in the focus. So, when one talks about the 'poor', and wants to do something about stark poverty that grips the lives of many all over the world, issues which are systemic, which are responsible for keeping the poor, poor need to be addressed. About nine million people die due to hunger every year[7], and this year, as a fallout of the COVID-19 pandemic the number is expected to double.

Querida Amazonia is also about the growing impoverishment of the poor, their cries, their rights. Pope Francis begins the part of the 'Social Dream' on the right note. He challenges one and all to have the courage to read and respond to the cries of the poor. Times have changed and we are called to make a paradigm-shift in our response. The traditional benefactor approach (which in the past was the hallmark of the response of the Church) is no longer accepted and will certainly not be an effective response for a change which is sustainable. We need to look into issues which are endemic (the root causes of poverty). This is all easier said than done – because in doing so we will have to take on the powerful and other vested interests; these could the Government, the corporate sector, and the mining mafia. Whether it is in the countries of the Amazon (as we see in The Mission) or in countries like India; when one confronts the powerful on behalf of the poor, means, with all certainty, that one has to pay a price. There are no short-cuts – we witness the downward spiral of how the poor become poorer and how the rich (at the cost of the poor) amass a scandalous amount of wealth. This is all far from the Gospel of Jesus and for that matter from Christian discipleship.

This reality takes place all over; the poor are treated with disdain as second-class citizens as if they have no rights. According to Global Multidimensional Poverty Index (MPI) 2020[8], India is 62nd among 107 countries with an MPI score of 0.123 and 27.91% headcount ratio, based on the NFHS 4 (2015/16) data. It is common knowledge that the poor are systematically exploited, denied just wages for long hours of work and they have no access to the 'fruits' of so-called development.

Several years ago, Mahatma Gandhi very prophetically said, "The earth has enough to satisfy every man's need but not every man's greed." These words are so true today. The growing economic inequalities are a major cause of concern. One needs to look around and to see the scandalous way in which the gap between the rich and the poor increases day by day. Franco-American activist, Susan George in her celebrated work in 1976 entitled, *How the Other Half Dies*[9], makes out a case of how a few across the world control the lives and destinies of the vast majority through unjust trade and other economic measures. Statistics can be reeled out ad nauseam to evidence this reality, but the fact is that 'greed' erodes the foundation of all that is good.

III.iii. The Ecological Crisis is about Human Rights

Laudato Si was the first major Papal teaching on a subject of critical importance namely, 'the environment'. In the opening statements of the Encyclical, Pope Francis makes his intention clear, "to address every person living on this planet" (#3). He says:

> This sister (mother earth) now cries out to us because of the harm we have inflicted on her by our irresponsible use and abuse of the goods with which God has endowed her. We have come to see ourselves as her lords and masters, entitled to plunder her at will. The violence present in our hearts wounded by sin, is also reflected in the symptoms of sickness evident in the soil, in the water, in the air and in all forms of life (#2).
> The same thoughts are expressed throughout *Querida Amazonia*.

In *Laudato Si*, Pope Francis states that, "We cannot adequately combat environmental degradation unless we attend to causes related to human and social degradation" (#48); he deals here with several 'aspects of the present ecological crisis' – pollution, waste and the throw-away culture; climate as a common good; displacement and migration caused by environmental degradation; access to safe drinking water as a basic and universal human right; loss of bio-diversity; decline in the quality of human life and break down of society; global inequality. He also denounces unequivocally the use of pesticides and the production of genetically engineered (GE) crops.

Pope Francis strongly notes that, "The earth's resources are also being plundered because of short-sighted approaches to the economy, commerce and production" (#32). He ensures that *Laudato Si* focuses on human rights violations and injustices. He does not mince words when he says:

> In the present condition of global society, where injustices abound and growing numbers of people are deprived of basic human rights and considered expendable, committing oneself to the common good means to make choices in solidarity based on a preferential option for the poorest of our brothers and sisters (#158).

We witness this grim reality unfolding in India today. Recently, the Ministry of Environment gave a green signal to more than forty projects without the mandatory environmental clearances. Most of these projects favour the rich crony capitalist friends of the Government, literally giving them a license to loot, plunder and rape the environment and much more! Precious biodiversity and our fragile ecosystems are being destroyed. The Government today just does not care and has clearly gone on a downward spiral, doing everything they can to destroy the environment. The destruction of the ecosystems in the Western Ghats and the Aravalli Hills, the building of a dam in Dibang, the selling of coal mines to private companies, the felling of thousands of trees to construct an unnecessary two-way rail track in Goa to profit a business magnate, the inter-linking of rivers in Gujarat to help industry, are but some of the blatantly anti-environmental policies of the Government.

Ramachandra Guha is one of India's foremost historians who also writes on a range of other subjects. Voicing his concern at the environmental crisis in his book, *Environmentalism: A Global History*[10], he says:

> The changes which the destruction of forests, the clearing of plants and the cultivation of indigo have produced within half a century in the quantity of water flowing in on the one hand, and on the other the evaporation of the soil and the dryness of the atmosphere, present causes sufficiently powerful to explain the successive diminution of the lake of Valencia . . . By felling the trees that cover the tops and sides

> of mountains, men in every climate prepare at once two calamities for future generations, the want of fuel and the scarcity of water.

Pope Francis says every section of society must play a definite role in a collaborative and concerted manner to address the ecological crisis. He challenges international and national governments and mechanisms saying,

> The same mindset which stands in the way of making radical decisions to reverse the trend of global warming also stands in the way of achieving the goal of eliminating poverty. A more responsible overall approach is needed to deal with both problems: the reduction of pollution and the development of poorer countries and regions (#175).

III. A Way Forward

The reality, one needs to admit, is extremely complex; the way forward is not easy, it is full of obstacles, besides there are no short-cuts. Given all this, it is imperative that all women and men of goodwill (particularly those who call themselves as 'disciples of Jesus') do all they can to right the wrongs. The possible ways of doing so could include:

- to study, reflect and analyse the realities which throttle the poor and marginalised (particularly the indigenous people/ the Adivasis) today; one needs to do substantial studies on the ways these people are exploited and oppressed and also on the fragile ecosystems they live in; besides one also needs to study their legitimate rights and the official policies
- to accompany these people (being in their midst) in their relentless quest for a more just and humane society; to engage in social dialogue with the different groups that are affected; to forge a sense of unity and purpose among them; to endeavour to find forms of communion and common struggle
- to network and collaborate with other like-minded groups and individuals; to join in public protests and rallies; to "hit the streets", in the words of Pope Francis
- to communicate to others the realities of the vulnerable, by engaging in advocacy, writing, speaking and using social media effectively

- to seek legal redress, whenever and wherever possible
- to take an uncompromising stand for truth and non-violence (ahimsa) in all our efforts in the way Jesus shows us to do so

Ultimately, the only way forward is to come to grips with the grim reality that overwhelms us and literally take 'the bull by the horns'. Arundhati Roy is one of India's most prolific writers in English. Her writings focus on contemporary reality. Well-known globally, she is also the recipient of the prestigious Booker Man Prize in literature. In her latest book, *Azadi*[11], she says:

> As we pass through this portal into another kind of world, we will have to ask ourselves what we want to take with us and what we will leave behind. We may not always have a choice - but not thinking about it will not be an option. And in order to think about it, we need an even deeper understanding of the world gone by, of the devastation we have caused to our planet and the deep injustice between fellow human beings that we have come to accept.

IV. Conclusion

In a review[12] of *The Mission*, film critics Frederic and Mary Ann Brussat write:

> *The Mission* depicts the challenge of conscience that confronts us all in a world convulsed by power, greed, and violence. Its power lies in the way it convinces us that the fierce conflict-ridden world we see on the screen is similar to the one in which we live today. At the same time, The Mission is a deeply moving film that reminds us of the vitality of love, the miracle of grace, and the transforming power of acts of conscience.

India's Nobel-winning poet laureate Rabindranath Tagore gives a clear direction in his poem 'Leave This Chanting'[13]:

> Leave this chanting and singing and telling of beads!
> Whom dost thou worship in this lonely dark
> corner of a temple with doors all shut?

Open thine eyes and see thy God is not before thee!
He is there where the tiller is tilling the hard ground
and where the path-maker is breaking stones.
He is with them in sun and in shower,
and his garment is covered with dust.
Put off thy holy mantle and even like him
come down on the dusty soil.
Come out of thy meditations and leave aside
thy flowers and incense!
What harm is there if thy clothes become
tattered and stained?
Meet him and stand by him in toil and
in sweat of thy brow.

Querida Amazonia is finally a challenge to make dreams into a reality for the indigenous people, for the poor, for the environment; to right the wrongs are indeed an Amazonia Gift!

Notes

1. https://en.wikipedia.org/wiki/The_Mission_(1986_film)
2. https://www.nytimes.com/1986/10/26/movies/the-mission-carries-a-message-from-past-to-present.html
3. http://www.vatican.va/content/francesco/en/apost_exhortations/documents/papa-francesco_esortazione ap_20200202_querida-amazonia.html
4. http://www.vatican.va/content/francesco/en/encyclicals/documents/papa-francesco_20150524_enciclica-laudato-si.html
5. Mohandas Karamchand Gandhi, The Story of My Experiments with Truth (Public Affairs Press of Washington DC, 1948)
6. http://press.vatican.va/content/salastampa/en/bollettino/pubblico/2020/06/13/200613d.html
7. https://www.theworldcounts.com/challenges/people-and-poverty/hunger-and-obesity/how-many-people-die-from-hunger-each-year
8. https://pib.gov.in/PressReleasePage.aspx?PRID=1651981#:~:text=According%20to%20Global%20MPI%202020,(2015%2F16)%20data
9. https://en.wikipedia.org/wiki/How_the_Other_Half_Dies#
10. Ramachandra Guha, Environmentalism: A Global History (Longman, New York, 2000)
11. Arundhati Roy, Azadi (Penguin General UK, 2020)
12. https://www.spiritualityandpractice.com/films/reviews/view/5042/the-mission
13. Rabindranath Tagore, Gitanjali: Song Offerings (Indian Society of London, 1912) Poem 11

Supporting Indigenous Peoples to Defend Amazonia

Birgit Weiler

The article describes the process that gave rise to the indigenous umbrella organisations and explains what gives them their potential for autonomous action in the face of neo-extractivism and neo-colonialism. It then sets out and explains the key demands of the first peoples of the Amazon region. In the process it also highlights the roles and demands of indigenous women's organisations. The second part of the article deals with the great importance of global solidarity networks in view of the extreme danger facing the Amazon region and its consequences for the first peoples in particular. This section also includes a theological reflection on the issue.

The article that follows is primarily, but not exclusively, written from the perspective of Peru, where I live and work. In Peru I have been for years in contact with the two first or indigenous peoples, the Awajún and Wampi, of the northern Amazon region. As a result of my work I was invited to take part in the Amazon synod held in Rome in 2019.

Strengthening indigenous organisations and networks

In the second half of the 20th century the first peoples of Peru's Amazon region began to form their own organisations to defend their territories and demand respect for their way of life. Similar processes took place in the other eight countries that share the Amazon region, sometimes simultaneously, sometimes a little later. Gradually the indigenous organisations in the Amazon region founded national umbrella organisations such as the Inter-Ethnic Development Association of the Peruvian Rainforest (AIDESEP), the Confederation of Indigenous Nations of the Ecuadorian Amazon (CONFENIAE), and the Coordinating Committee of Indigenous Organisations of the Brazilian Amazon (COIAB).

The umbrella organisations at national level are very important for the indigenous peoples, as they constantly represent their interests and wishes vis à vis the state. Frequently they are the most important dialogue partners of the state authorities on topics such as the protection of indigenous territories and the collective rights of indigenous people. In case where the rights of indigenous communities are being violated, a frequent occurrence, the national coalitions can be more effective in getting a hearing from the relevant state authorities and society in support of their demands for full respect of these rights. Often they give emphatic reminders of the first peoples' demands for an alternative to the dominant economic model, largely based on the unrestrained exploitation of natural resources, and for this purpose set up networks of solidarity and cooperation with international non-indigenous organisations. The various national coalitions are united in the Coordinating Committee of the Indigenous Organisations of the Amazon Basin (COICA), the largest international coalition of indigenous organisation in the whole Amazon basin. COICA is an important dialogue partner of the Church Panamazonian Network, REPAM.

The need for networking in the face of growing threats from neo-extractivism[1] and neocolonialism

The indigenous peoples in the Amazon region are currently discovering that the Amazonian biosphere is being damaged on an increasingly large scale by the cumulative and mutually reinforcing effects of the numerous projects to exploit both renewable and non-renewable raw materials.

Many of these activities are being carried out in the traditional territories of the indigenous people, not infrequently without the prior consultation prescribed by law. The economy in the Amazon that is based primarily on extractivism and export has many negative consequences for the lives of the indigenous communities. Their territories are increasingly ecologically damaged and destroyed. Various scientists, such as Carlos Nobre, the Brazilian expert on ecological systems and climate change in the Amazon region, and his team are warning, on the basis of their research findings, that in some areas the Amazon region is approaching an irreversible tipping point and risks becoming savannah. This would have catastrophic consequences for the water resources and the ecosystems of the region and for the climate, not only in Amazonia and Latin America, but also worldwide. The Amazon region is a clear example of the way neo-extractivism and neocolonialism affect and reinforce each other.

The demand for protection of territories, a government of their own and autonomy

Among indigenous peoples life is 'is inserted into, linked with and integrated in territory'.[2] In addition the ecological conditions set limits to human activity as people interact with the fragile ecosystems of the territory. From their experiences and the wisdom they have acquired in the course of various generations and handed down, the indigenous peoples know that everything is connected with everything else and forms a 'vital whole'.[3] Human beings must therefore learn to live alongside the earth and the other species, and not at their expense through unlimited consumption. At the same time, the territories are 'a social and legal construction aiming at autonomy'.[4] Leaders and organisations of the indigenous peoples fight by democratic means to have their constitutional rights respected by the various states who have accepted this commitment by signing the relevant international agreements. They demand that they, members of indigenous peoples, should be recognised in practice as enjoying rights, possessing collective rights such as the right to free self-determination, to territory as collective property, and to political participation and a say in decisions that affect the life and future of their communities. Here it is also important to bear in mind the cross-connections that exist between these rights. The indigenous organisations have seen this very clearly and express it in the close connection between their demands for collective property, a government of their own, self-government and autonomy. In this way they want to protect their territories from fragmentation through the granting of ever more concessions to firms from the extractive sector of the economy, and to prevent their territories from finally being taken from them completely. The defence of the territories involves questions of power, because the indigenous peoples do not want to be disempowered in their territories by other actors who try in practice to force their model of the extractive economy on them. Instead, the indigenous communities want to retain control of their territories and the natural resources in them. There are interested in an ecologically responsible 'use of common goods'.[5]

In Thomas Fatheuer's words, territory and rights are the 'starting point and core' of resistance to the dominant economic and development model,[6] and of the commitment to self-determined models of life and economic activity by the indigenous communities. If they are to defend their territories against the enormous pressure of the big extractive and export-oriented economic projects and the associated development model in the Amazon region, the indigenous organisations need not only good networking among themselves at regional, national and international level, but also international solidarity networks with other, non-indigenous actors.

Indigenous women organise in response to climate change

Women from various indigenous peoples are joining together to stress that, especially in rural areas, in general it is women who are most affected by climate change and its catastrophic effects. 'Our sons and daughters are getting ill, our family economy is suffering from climate change, our fields are getting flooded, there are no harvests, and we have nothing to feed our children with.'[7] To counter this, in many countries of Latin America indigenous women have formed their own organisations, in Peru, for example, the National Organisation of Andean and Amazonian Women (ONAMIAP, 2009). It regards itself as an organisation in which women from indigenous peoples can make their voices heard, voices 'that for many years have been silenced'.[8] The women are calling for effective action against climate change and a non-extractive, ecologically responsible management of their territories. Since all areas of their lives are being affected by climate change, they are demanding, through their organisations, that indigenous women are also brought into the negotiations on climate policy in view of climate change.

The COICA indigenous coalition and the Church Panamazonian Network (REPAM), allies against climate change

In December 2018 COICA and REPAM concluded a cooperation agreement committing themselves to work together and with other actors to defend Amazonia as a living space. The collaboration takes place primarily in the defence of human rights and the collective rights of the indigenous people, including prior consultation in the case of projects that have effects on their territory and their lives. Both networks attempt to mount effective opposition jointly to the threats from extractivism and the hostility experienced by men and women, many of them from indigenous communities, who try, often at the cost of their lives, to protect the territory and the rainforest. This includes legal support for those who are falsely accused of illegal acts in connection with their commitment. COICA and REPAM also cooperate intensively on public information. In this they take particular care to ensure that members of indigenous communities and other marginalised population groups in the Amazon region can make their voices heard and that the indigenous organisations have a platform to make their concerns and wishes known to a broad national and international public. The agreement has reinforced the work of both organisations, intensified inter-cultural dialogue, and guaranteed the long-term effect of projects and socio-cultural processes that have been started.

Already many joint training courses have been run on topics such as human rights, the collective rights of indigenous peoples and the legal resources available to defend them. Among the participants there have been many young people who are now active multipliers.

Updated information about the pandemic in the Amazon region

The pandemic has intensified still further the cooperation between COICA and REPAM. Both organisations decided to produce a regular joint information sheet about the effects of COVID-19 among the indigenous peoples of the Panamazonian region to make their situation visible at national and international level and to appeal for solidarity. These data are the basis for practical acts of solidarity. For this purpose COICA and REPAM regularly produce a letter with the latest information. This information reveals the historic marginalisation of the indigenous peoples, the great social inequalities, in both number and quality, of the public health services, and the generally thin presence of the state in the region.

Amazonia matters to us all – the importance of global solidarity networks

In the face of the 'single socio-environmental crisis' unfolding in the Amazon,[9], the indigenous peoples and their organisations are well aware that the causes of the crisis can only be overcome through worldwide solidarity and shared responsibility for the future of the Amazon region. The global interconnections of ecological, socio-political and economic problems require a joint worldwide engagement to maintain the living space that is Amazonia. Networking on a global scale between the numerous organisations that share this concern is absolutely necessary, and in fact already exists. The indigenous actors in the numerous organisations and networks are campaigning for the protection of their territories and their rainforest in the knowledge that this is not just about a good future for their peoples, but about the wellbeing of the earth and the whole human family. It is well known that because of its extensive rainforests and high biodiversity Amazonia has an important function in the regulation of the climate throughout the world and of the earth's water resources. We therefore have to echo the voices of the indigenous organisations and insist that Amazonia matters to us all and requires a response from us. There is also a direct connection between the grave ecological and social problems in the Amazon region and the type of economy, lifestyle and consumption in the rich industrialised countries of the global North, including therefore Europe.

A large part of the resources obtained from the Amazon region through extractivism are exported to the rich industrial countries. Noteworthy examples are the export of tropical hardwoods, large quantities of minerals needed for digital technology, meat and animal fodder, for the production of which large areas of the rainforest are cleared, to be transformed into pasture or plantations of monocultures. Often to extract raw materials chemicals such as mercury are used, especially in illegal goldmining, or pesticides as in agribusiness. Firms that operate internationally have an urgent obligation to show a greater duty of care as regards respect for human rights and the maintenance of higher environmental standards, transparency in firms' contracts and practices. This means an effective law governing raw material supply chains in the countries of the global North and international solidarity with the indigenous peoples and their organisations vis-à-vis states and businesses, to ensure that they respect the collective rights of these peoples and carry out the statutory consultation processes transparently and observe the legal requirements.

In alliance with the indigenous peoples

At the Amazon Synod the Catholic Church accepted the request of the indigenous peoples and committed itself to an alliance with them in defence of the rights of the peoples and in the defence of nature against encroaching destruction. This requires a common effort to ensure that 'their words, their hopes and their fears should be the most authoritative voice at any table of dialogue on the Amazon region' (Pope Francis, Post-synodal Apostolic Exhortation *Querida Amazonía* ('Beloved Amazonia'), 26).[10] It requires solidarity networks at international level to get these demands implemented. In the spirit of Jesus and the 'preferential option on behalf of the poor, the marginalized and the excluded' (QA 27) implied by discipleship of Jesus, we must, as the Church, unite with the indigenous peoples, their organisations and networks to press for their views on what *buen vivir*, 'living well', looks like for themselves and their descendants to be central in any discussions.

The organisations and networks of the first peoples of the Amazon region are calling for an economic model that is viable ecologically, socially and culturally. Their fiercest criticism is directed at the capitalist economic model as they experience it in their region. They regard this way of managing the economy as one of the main causes of our serious social and ecological problems. In the wide-ranging debates that also take place among indigenous organisations, there are various positions on the question whether capitalism can be reformed or whether a completely new economic system is required. Within the scope of this article it is not possible to explain the different positions in detail. However, from the perspective of Christian social ethics we may note the critical view of Matthias Möhring-Hesse that 'the capitalist mode of economy and its inherent tendency to growth is one reason why the environment is exploited and burdened by production and consumption to a degree that far exceeds its capacity to cope with its exploitation and its burdens and to regenerate'.[11] That is why the indigenous peoples are against an extractive model of economy.

The need for a 'cultural revolution' (*Laudato Si'* 114)[12]

In the indigenous organisations and networks, and in the networks they are connected with internationally, there is a clear awareness that the maintenance of the rich biodiversity and complex ecosystems in Amazonia and on our whole planet urgently requires 'a bold cultural revolution' or a 'great transformation'.[13] Here networks as part of civil society play an important part. For the first peoples their comprehensive concept of *buen vivir*, 'living well', which is always connected with *buen hacer*, 'acting well' in the ethical sense, is an important source of inspiration and motivation for practising a comprehensive ecology, which is an essential element of cultural transformation. The comprehensive approach is ever present in *buen vivir,* as this is always about sharing the world both with other human beings and with other species and nature as a whole. In the mentality of these peoples 'living well' is not the same as having and earning more and more, but means what gives life meaning, happiness in life and inner peace. This connects it with values such as solidarity, community and the common good, and further with the careful use of common goods. The indigenous organisations realise that the coherent practice of the values associated with *buen vivir* are also now a constant challenge for the indigenous peoples under more difficult socio-cultural conditions.

The idea of life enshrined in *buen vivir* has many possible connections with other cultures. In many solidarity networks in the global North people have therefore translated central elements of the indigenous 'living well' into the circumstances of their own lives and share the idea that 'having a good life doesn't mean having lots of things',[14] or getting more and more and 'constantly increasing consumption'.[15] Many people experience meaning and joy in life in a simple lifestyle, part of which is the 'art of reduction',[16] in other words, a deliberate and freely chosen response to the flood of consumption and the massive, ever faster use of raw materials and energy resources, which are largely mined or otherwise produced at the expense of human beings and nature. They share the conviction expressed in the final document of the Amazon synod,[17] originally with reference to the Amazon region but equally valid for the whole of our Earth ecosystem, that we urgently need and integral ecology to save the Amazon region and our planet. This also provides the basis for taking responsibility for creation in practice.

Protecting common goods in networks

As Christians we are called to hear 'both the cry of the earth and the cry of the poor' (Pope Francis, *Laudato Si'*, 49). This applies particularly to Amazonia; we are called to respond in solidarity and shared responsibility for this region, wherever we live. This faces us with a central topic in the practice of our Christian faith. God has entrusted creation to us as a gift of his love. God's love is for all his creatures; the whole of creation is dear to him. The indigenous peoples remind us that we are a part of this earth and so must act with ecological responsibility and care. The vital goods of this earth are common goods, intended for all people and not just a few Among these common goods is the climate. In networks with indigenous organisations we can campaign together on various levels for this principle to be recognised and observed more strictly than hitherto.

The COVID-19 pandemic has shown once more that everything is connected with everything else, and that a healthy life is not possible on a sick earth. María Neira, Director of the Department of Public Health and Environment at the World Health Organization (WHO), has pointed out that 70% of the outbreaks of recent epidemics have begun with the felling of forests, and has explained how, as in the cases of Ebola, SARS and HIV, the virus has passed from animals to human beings.[18]

Networks and finding alternatives

Networks inspired by solidarity and a shared responsibility for the good of the human family can be important catalysts for the processes of cultural transformation we need. The Panamazonian Social Forum (FOSPA) is a sign of fruitful collaboration between indigenous organisations and many other networks in Amazonia and the global North. It provides for a exchange of learning experiences and ideas as part of the process of finding practicable alternatives to extractivism. Work in international solidarity networks makes it possible 'to overcome the various colonising mentalities' (*Querida Amazonía*, 17) and meet on equal terms in a common commitment to a good future for Amazonia and its peoples. From Christians this demands openness to God's Spirit, which 'blows where it chooses' (Jn 3.8), and thus for ecumenical, interfaith and intercultural dialogue.

Translated by Francis McDonagh

Notes

1. What has become known as extractivism has been practised as far back as the colonial period and continues today, adapted to current socio-political and economic conditions (hence the name 'neo-extractivism'). On this, see Gerhard Kruip's article in this issue of Concilium.
2. Amazonia: New Paths for the Church and for an Integral Ecology: Working Document of the Synod of Bishops for the Special Assembly for the Pan-Amazon Region, 17 June 2019, para. 19. http://www.synod.va/content/sinodoamazonico/en/documents/pan-amazon-synod--the-working-document-for-the-synod-of-bishops.html
3. Working Document, para. 21.
4. Thomas Fatheuer, Amazonien heute. Eine Region zwischen Entwicklung, Zerstörung und Klimaschutz (Heinrich Böll Stiftung, Schriften zur Ökologie, vol. 46), Berlin, 2019, p. 54.
5. Thomas Fatheuer, Amazonien heute. Eine Region zwischen Entwicklung, Zerstörung und Klimaschutz, p. 60.
6. Fatheuer, p. 60.
7. Ana Lucía Núñez and Nelly Romero, Mujeres indígenas frente a la agenda climática en el Perú, in: http://peru.oxfam.org/latest/blogs/mujeres-ind%C3%ADgenas-frente-la-agenda-clim%C3%A1tica-en-el-per%C3%BA, accessed 03/08/2021
8. ONAMIAP, in: http://onamiap.org/nuestra-historia/, accessed 05/08/2021.
9. Amazon Synod, Final Document, 10: https://www.vatican.va/roman_curia/synod/documents/rc_synod_doc_20191026_sinodo-amazzonia_en.html
10. Pope Francis' post-synodal Apostolic Exhortation Querida Amazonía is available at: http://www.synod.va/content/sinodoamazonico/en/documents/post-synodal-apostolic-exhortation--querida-amazonia-.html
11. Matthias Möhring-Hesse, 'Introduction', in: Matthias Möhring-Hesse, Bernhard Emunds and Judith Hahn (eds), Friedhelm Hengsbach, Entgifteter Kapitalismus – faire Demokratie. Texte zur Reform von Kirche, Wirtschaft und Gesellschaft, Ostfildern, 2013, pp 329-331, quotation from p. 331.
12. Pope Francis, Laudato Si'. On the Care of the Common Home (24 May 2015): https://www.vatican.va/content/francesco/en/encyclicals/documents/papa-francesco_20150524_enciclica-laudato-si.html
13. Uwe Scheidewind, Die Große Transformation. Eine Einführung in die Kunst gesellschaftlichen Wandels, Frankfurt am Main, 2018.
14. Gerhard Kruip and Birgit Weiler, 'Was wir von Amazonien lernen können. Ein theologischer Ort', Herder Korrespondenz 10 (2019), 13–15, quotation from p. 15.
15. Gerhard Kruip and Birgit Weiler, 'Was wir von Amazonien lernen können. Ein theologischer Ort'.
16. Niko Paech, 'Maßvolle Lebensstile. Lob der Reduktion', politische ökologie 135 (2013), 16–22, quotation from p. 16.
17. Amazon Synod, Final Document, 66: https://www.vatican.va/roman_curia/synod/documents/rc_synod_doc_20191026_sinodo-amazzonia_en.html
18. Vgl. María Neira, 'El 70% de los últimos brotes epidémicos han comenzado con la deforestación', https://elpais.com/ciencia/2021-02-05/el-70-de-los-ultimos-brotes-epidemicos-han-comenzado-con-la-deforestacion.html.

Part Three: Reflection on the Issue

A New Look at Creation Theology From Amazonia

Fernando Roca Alcázar SJ

In the meeting of catholic theology and the religious beliefs of Amazonian tribes, the relationship with nature plays a major role. The proposal for a pneumatological doctrine of creation such as that put forward by Moltmann may well be an important element in opening up an inter-faith dialogue with a specific Amazonian tribe: the Awajún-Wampis.

The Pope Francis' stance on the theme of the environment has appeared in his pontificate from his adoption of his name as Francis, in homage to the saint of Assisi, patron saint of Ecology. Subsequently in his encyclical *Laudato Sí* and, finally, in the celebration of the Amazonian Synod, the first in the history of the Church related to an ecosystem, one with probably the most abundant number of life forms on the planet. Amazonia, the greatest biomass of tropical forests on earth, with immense hydro resources, the ancestral home of many peoples whose origins lie in Latin America and a point of confluence for a wide range of cultures drawn from other continents. For its indigenous peoples the relationship between man and nature forms part of their identity. Their experience of religion is linked to nature, to space and to the earth. The key necessities that sustain are linked to nature: water, rain, shelter, food, materials to clothe them, heat, light, fire, medicines, beliefs. Consequently, the earth, nature and creation have a special dimension for them, in many cases linked to sacred space. Fortunately, modern man is beginning to realise the importance of respect for and a sustainable use of nature, that we have a relationship of dependency on it. It can carry on its evolutional journey without us, we cannot exist without it. The encyclical *Laudato Sí* affirms that all things are related[1] and because of this proposes an "integral ecology" as the response to a "…sole and complex socioenvironmental crisis",[2] the responsibility for which falls principally on us, human beings.

Taking this reading of the relationships of human beings with nature as a point of reference, I would like to show how a Theology of Creation as proposed by Jurgen Moltmann in his work *God in Creation*[3] can be inspirational in a theological dialogue with the religious beliefs of the Amazonian indigenous peoples. While it is true that Leonardo Boff was one of the pioneers in Latin America to talk of eco-theology, linking the cries of the poor to those of the earth[4], Moltmann's work although it dates from the end of the last century, remains valid in a pioneering sense in daring to propose a pneumatological reading for the theology of creation. We need to build bridges for a Theology of Creation to enable a dialogue with these peoples that can establish a relation with the natural world that structures their lives, their cultural universe, their experience of the supernatural, their ways of understanding themselves and the world that surrounds them.

In recent papal documents and writings, such as the encyclical *Laudato Sí*[5], the Synodical Document *Amazonía: Nuevos caminos para la Iglesia y para una ecología integral*[6] and in his Apostolic Exhortation *Querida Amazonía*[7], we also find a call to rediscover this new way of linking ourselves to nature, to reshape our dialogue with creation. How can we establish touch points in this new form of "linking ourselves to nature" as expressed by the peoples of Amazonia?

I. The "environmental treaty of creation" by Jürgen Moltmann

The German protestant theologian, Jürgen Moltmann, tells us in his work on creation that the environmental crisis is a crisis for mankind.[8] We can find here a clear similarity with the subsequently written encyclical *Laudato Sí.*[9] The author, from a standpoint of theology, proposes a pneumatical doctrine of creation in order better to understand mankind's relationship with nature: "This doctrine, arising from creation being inhabited by the divine spirit, offers starting points for discussions with natural philosophers that are integral in character, not mechanistic, and are as old as they are modern."[10]

The German theologian affirms that the knowledge of nature as a creation of God is an interactive one. This is a contribution that we can take in considering the indigenous peoples and their relationship with nature in seeking a theology that calls for interreligious dialogue. We need to leave behind the notion of subject-object relationships. The relationship between man and nature needs to be thought of in new ways based upon a model of reciprocal communication and integration. You have to have knowledge in order to share and not to dominate.[11] Here we find common ground with the thinking of the indigenous peoples, defined as a way of thinking that both integrates with and shares in the worlds that surround them.[12] For those who seek a meeting point with the indigenous peoples of Amazonia, this approach is enriching, proposing, as it does, an interactive relationship, a feeling of being part of nature and one of dominance.

The various Amazonian peoples have established an interactive relationship with nature because they are conscious that they are a part of it. Their wonder faced with what nature shows them suggests that there has been an initial moment of awareness of the knowledge of the creation of which they are part and which surrounds them. Aristotle affirmed that wonder was the gateway to knowledge. This is not simply utilitarian knowledge, quite the contrary. One cannot know the purpose of something without understanding what it is. Nature should be respected because we are linked it it and it to us (and this affirmation is not only true for the indigenous peoples: western society is equally linked to nature although it has frequently lost its sense of direction and its awareness of this connection). While it is certain that nature does not need mankind to continue its process of evolution, humans can have a defining influence in this, something, in fact, we are doing. It is interesting to remark that if we cut our relationship with nature, objectifying it, we are also cutting our relationship with our own bodies, which are part of it. There is a mysterious and complex dynamic which binds us together, as the Pope has affirmed, "For all creatures are connected….", "Everything is related…", "…. intimately related".[13]

Christianity deepens and intensifies this perspective. In the light of Jesus Christ, this creation is oriented towards the glory of the fulfilment of the messianic times, the glory of creation, called by Moltmann ,"a community of creation". [14]

A misreading of "fill the earth and subdue it. Rule over the fish in the sea and the birds in the sky and over every living creature that moves on the ground." (Gen. 1,28) has contributed to the present environmental crisis. This incorrect interpretation supposes a rupture between the three fundamental relationships which appear in the Book of Genesis: the relationship with God, with one's neighbour and with the earth. A rupture that is understood as a sin and which presumes a breakdown between these three relationships… through a desire to be like God (LS66; Gen 3,5). There is a need to develop a new interpretation based on what nature means to us, how we are part of it and the relationships that we establish with it, understanding it as a divine creation, knowing how to learn to live with it (Gen 2,15), in it, with it, with others and with all of creation.[15] Only in this way can we "avoid distancing it" as a simple object over which we can assume control. As human beings we have become accustomed to dominating nature, exhausting or destroying its resources. We have put nature's resilience to the test and, in many case, its capacity for renewal has not been able to respond sufficiently: hundreds possibly thousands of vanished species; oceans, lakes and rivers, polluted; woodlands converted to pasture for livestock, to agricultural plantations, some specialists talk of the appearance of vast plains or huge single farms where once there stood dense tropical forests, all of this a product of human intervention. The Climate Change which we are living through reminds us of this. Fortunately, we have both experience and proposals that seek either to recover or strengthen the resilience that exists within creation, within nature. Some of these are the maintenance of "standing forests", the recovery of degraded land and the decontamination of seas, lakes and rivers. We evidence this as human beings when we collaborate with nature in those tasks which in some instances we classify as "restoration"[16] and in others as "sustainable development". Nature responds generously when we provide conditions which allow it to take back what has been taken away. Considering this, creation remains alive despite all hopes to the contrary. As human beings we need to cultivate this "universal brotherly dependence" not only with each other but also with our "Shared home". A relationship which should also encompass simple spaces for prayer, reflection and dialogue. This is where "Ignation Contemplation" as outlined by St Ignatius de Loyola in his Spiritual Exercises acquires a very real and relevant dimension. All of this is and needs to be very present in an Amazonian spirituality.

In this context, theology has something to say about this in terms of its relationship with natural sciences. We are talking here of a theology of nature, or more exactly of a theology of creation where the Creator is present and interacting with "his creation". A theology of creation that supports the process of mankind and creation's (nature) integration, because mankind is also "creation". God's imprint exists as much in the human condition as it does in creation. We can ask ourselves in what way, since God is in everything. This question and the search for an answer, can be helpful to us faced with a straightforward acceptance of a pantheistic vision in which a divine, supernatural force, is present in the same way in all things. Pantheism takes us further from a catholic theology imbued with the Trinity of the father, Son and Holy Spirit.

II. The workings of the Holy Spirit and its relationship with the Amazonian peoples

> Creation exists in the Spirit, is impregnated through the Son and is created by the Father. It is, thus, from God, through God and in God. The trinitarian concept of creation links the transcendence of God with his immanence in the world.[17]

In affirming this, Moltmann links a trinitarian theology of creation with what we mentioned at the outset as a pneumatical doctrine of creation. The immanence and transcendence of God appear as two constituent elements of our being part of nature and of our relation with it.

Amazonian religions generally hold that nature is peopled by spirits which live both in living things and often in inanimate ones as well. How to establish an approach that supposes both a break and a continuity at the same time, when a trinitarian theology of creation starts a dialogue with them? How, also, to talk of a pneumatical doctrine of creation? How to demonstrate the difference between pantheism as it is seen by these religions and the announcement of the Good News, of a God present in everything, but in different ways in each thing? In the case of this dialogue with the indigenous peoples here is a challenge if the telling of the Good News that catholic theology offers to all of us. How to evangelise without uprooting and entire local oral tradition, impregnated with a religious dimension that forms a constituent part of these ancient peoples of Amazonia? It is here that that the trajectory or evolutionary process of the patient communication and revelation, teaching and love of the Creative Spirit is really important. This is the path we are on and we shall progress forward as we walk, revelation remains valid in all and in creation. The Seeds of the Word are so much more than mere seeds.

Amongst the indigenous Awajún and Wampis peoples (part of the Jíbaro ethnolinguistic group of the Peruvian Amazon), the understanding of the Holy Spirit had apparently been well received. Following many years of pastoral work by the Silesian Mission with the Jíbaro Shuar in Ecuador and the Jesuit Mission with the Wampis in Peru, the Holy Spirit in the Awajún language has been translated as *Wakaní Pegkeji,* the Good Spirit. The concept of a saint or of saintliness does not exist in the Jíbaro tongue. However, what does the concept of *Wakán* mean in Awajún?

"*Wakán* in the Awajún language is a word with multiple meanings. At times it can mean the image of a person on the water; at others his shadow. The spirits of the dead that appear in dreams, often in the shape of animals are also called *wakán*. In these same dreams, the person's *wakán* will make their name known. During the dream, the *wakán* leaves the body and visits the places where they have been; on other occasions they might prophesy future events. *Wakán* and *Iwanch* are used indiscriminately to designate those who have died. Animals and plants also have their *wakán*. When *baikóa* (Stramonium datura, an entheogenic plant – author's note) is taken to generate visions, the hallucinogenic plant's *wakán* takes the drugged young person to a place of safety, keeping them from potential dangers; similarly, it is the *wakán* of the *tsúak* plant that tells the patient which illness that is being experienced and what are the most appropriate remedies."[18]

As can be appreciated, there is a possibility of understanding the *Wakaní Pegkeji* in a pantheistic way linking it with the "spirits that inhabit the "Amazonian jungle" and at the same time believe that the action and strength of the Holy Spirit are present. Nevertheless, it is here that we can establish the difference between them in making clear "the ways in which God exists in all things". In his Spiritual Exercises (SE), St Ignatius of Loyola in reflecting on what he establishes as the "Fourth Week" (SE 230-237), proposes that the student initially brings to mind the benefits received from God (EE234), and then:

> [235] Secondly, to look at how God lives in all creatures, in the elements giving life, in the plants giving growth, in the animals giving sensation, in human kind giving understanding; and so within myself giving me being, life, sense and enabling me to understand; similarly making a temple of me as made in the likeness and image of his divine majesty; reflecting as much on myself in the ways set out in the first point, or in another which I might consider to be better.
> [236] Thirdly, to consider how God works and labours for me in all things created in the face of the earth, i.e. habet se ad modum laborantis (i.e. behaves like one who labours). Such as the heavens, the elements, plants, fruit, livestock and so forth, giving being, conserving, growing, sensing and so on. And then, reflect this in myself.[19]

There is a proposition for God's presence in all things created, but at the same time it is in the human condition where God's work shows itself most particularly and differently from the rest of creation. This is due to the incarnation of God in Jesus, taking on our human form. Here we find the Christlike dimension, a constituent part of the trinitarian theology of creation with God the Father and God the Holy Spirit.

Moltmann starts with the divine Spirit (*ruah*) as a creative force and the presence of God in creation. This Spirit is revealed in the history of salvation and in the experiences of the "Holy Spirit" in the community of Christ. It is from this perspective, through the actions of the "Spirit" in creation, that we understand the presence and the world.[20]
As Moltmann says:

> The trinitarian concept of creation links the transcendence of God in the world with his immanence. The unilateral emphasis on the transcendence of God with regard to the world led to deism, as in the case of Newton. The unilateral emphasis on the immanence of God with regard to the world led to pantheism – as was the case with Spinoza. In the trinitarian concept of creation there is an integral truth that contains both monotheism and pantheism. In the pantheistic vision, the God who created the world lives within it, and the world created by God exists within it. This pantheistic vision is only conceivable and representable

in terms of trinitarianism.[21]

Through dialogue with animistic religions we can show how, while it is true that God's workings are in all creation, in the human condition this is only manifest through the mystery of the Incarnation. This does not suggest an "absence" of God in the rest of creation, but rather of a differentiated presence, the Father's pneumatical workings make it possible that all is duly linked together. This is something that Pope Francis repeatedly affirms. The pantheism proposed by Moltmann (the differentiation of God's presence in all things) makes a dialogue possible. Is this sufficient to enable an evangelising offer without falling into contradictions within our own theology?

We can seek the answer from Moltmann himself:

> Yet differentiated pantheism is incapable of combining the transcendence of God with respect to the world with the immanence of God within the world. This is the advantage of the trinitarian doctrine of creation in the Spirit, and by the Spirit of the Creator who lives within creation. This doctrine considers consideration as a dynamic fabric of interdependent processes. The Spirit both differentiates and links. The Spirit sustains and enables living beings and communities to transcend themselves. This Spirit of the Creator that dwells in creation is fundamental to the communion of creation.[22]

A final element of Moltmann's work that I would like to consider is the importance of the heaven-earth binomial, showing a link to the religion-nature binomial. This link is critical in the dialogue with the Amazonian people's religions. The heaven-earth dual concept, with heaven seen as the dominion of God's possibilities and creative strength, the earth as the dominion of the created reality and its intrinsic possibilities, can be understood as a binary world, but in which we can find an intimate relationship between heaven and earth. Heaven is open to God, and through this opening, the world has a future. God's reign is accomplished in both heaven and earth.

From this approach, the relationship between religion and nature becomes clearer. In their experience of the sacred, the indigenous peoples have succeeded in integrating the heaven-earth binomial in an intimate relationship with that of religion and nature. Nevertheless, if heaven is considered as the locus of the divine, it is not the only one. The seas, the waters, the deeps, night and darkness are also places with a godly presence. The author's observation is that as soon as the relationship heaven-earth disappears, people get into crisis. We need to ask ourselves whether Christianity can help traditional religions to articulate this relationship better in their own faiths. A Christianity that profanes creation (and nature) deconsecrating it for various reasons will not be aware of this dimension for the indigenous peoples and, so, will be incapable of inculturating it.

III. By way of a conclusion

In conclusion, it is the creative force of the Spirit that has built the Church. It is also present in creation and in nature. Nevertheless, there is no question about the presence of this force in the Church or nature - its presence is manifest. The question does arise in the manner in which it is present. For the world of indigenous Amazonians it is here where question becomes fundamental for an understanding of the trinitarian mystery: you cannot take away the creative force of the Spirit that works in nature (for example, in a plant), but you cannot attribute to nature alone the entirety of the presence of the Spirit. How to set free the workings of the Spirit in both mankind and in the natural indigenous world?.... It is only with time and the workings of the Spirit through the process of evangelising (evangelisers and evangelised) that we will be shown the way.

Translated by Christopher Lawrence

Notes

1. Papa Francisco, Laudato Sí. Sobre el cuidado de la casa común. Roma: Librería Editrice Vaticana. 2015, n. 42, 137.
2. Laudato Si', n. 139.
3.Jürgen Moltmann, Dios en la creación. Doctrina ecológica de la creación. Salamanca: Sígueme, 1987.
4. Leonardo Boff, Dignitas terrae: ecologia: grito da terra, grito dos pobres. São Paulo: Ática, 1995.
5. Papa Francisco, Laudato Si, Carta Encíclica sobre el cuidado de la casa común. Lima: Ed. Paulinas, Lima, 2015.

6. http://www.synod.va/content/sinodoamazonico/es/documentos/documento-final-de-la-asamblea-especial-del-sinodo-de-los-obispo.pdf consulted 28 October 2020
7.http://www.vatican.va/content/francesco/es/apost_exhortations/documents/papa-francesco_esortazione-ap_20200202_querida-amazonia.pdf , consulted 28 October 2020
8.Jürgen Moltmann, Dios en la creación, 1987, p. 9.
9. Laudato Si', n. 139.
10. Jürgen Moltmann, Dios en la creación, 1987, p. 10
11. Idem, p. 16-17.
12. Claude Lévi-Strauss, La Pensée Sauvage, París, Librairie Plon, 1962, particularly in Ch.II, La logique des classifications totémiques.
13. Laudato Si', n. 42, 92, 137.
14. Jürgen Moltmann, Dios en la creación, 1987, p. 19.
15. Papa Francisco, Carta encíclica Fratelli Tutti. On fraternity and social friendships. Lima, Ed. Paulinas, octubre 2020, n. 1-2.
16. Cf. J. Aronson & A. F. Clewell, Ecological restoration. Principles, Values and Structure of an Emerging Profession. Washington, Covelo, London: Island Press, Second Edition, 2013.
17. Jürgen Moltmann, Dios en la creación, 1987, p. 111.
18. Lucia Aurelio Chumap / Manuel García-Rendueles, Duik Muun, Universo Mítico de los Aguaruna, Vol. II, Centro Amazónico de Antropología y Aplicación Práctica, Serie Antropológica II, Lima, Perú, 1979, p. 800
19. Ignacio de Loyola, Ejercicios Espirituales, Santander, Sal Terrae, 1987, p. 135.
20. Jürgen Moltmann, Dios en la creación, 1987, p. 112.
21. Idem, p. 111.
22. Idem, p. 117.
23. Idem, p. 173-198.

Gift and Task: From Differentiation to Solidarity

Cristino Robles Pine

Pope Francis challenges everyone to establish networks of solidarity to advance human dignity and the environment, respecting diversity. He considers the Amazon region as a theological locus. In connection with this, we know that Genesis 1:28 and its dominant interpretation has been for a long time used to justify human beings abuse of the natural world. This paper, through a reader-oriented intertextuality, with "light" and "darkness" as keywords, offers an alternative way of reading Genesis 1:1–2:3 with Job 29:1-25. This reading highlights differentiation as God's gift to creation and solidarity as a human task.

In his Encyclical *Laudato Si'*, Pope Francis summons everyone to urgently care for our common home, transforming the one-dimensional and undifferentiated technocratic paradigm. To do so is to live out an essential part of Christian faith. Moreover, in his Exhortation *Querida Amazonia*, Pope Francis is apparently suggesting to take the Amazon region as a theological locus. The Amazon region, characterized by cultural richness and abundant biodiversity, now faces threats to human dignity and environment. Recognizing the beauty of diversity, Pope Francis boldly dreams of a holiness with Amazonian features that can challenge the universal Church. Thus, the abovementioned documents advocate to establish networks of solidarity for the protection of both human dignity and the natural environment.[1] Committed Christians are challenged to participate in this solidarity project that upholds the value of diversity. The biblical texts can contribute to the building up of such networks of solidarity. To cite, however, the dominant reading of Genesis 1:28 has, for a long time, justified human beings' destructive domination of the natural world. This paper offers an alternative reading of the differentiation of light and darkness in two selected biblical texts containing creation motif, which may contribute to the ongoing search for a biblically-based creation theology.

I. Reader-Oriented Intertextuality

R. S. Sugirtharajah explains that before the western interpretations of biblical texts became normative, the texts were marginal. The Bible was first propagated before Europe became a political and cultural colonial power. In the course of history, western interpretations dominated the discipline of biblical theological readings. Hence, the biblical texts must be set free from the hegemony of western interpretations. Furthermore, postcolonial critics see the need for the biblical texts to emancipate from their association with dominant and homogenizing ideologies. Colonial ideologies must first be detected should the Bible emancipate from such ideologies not only at the interpretive level but also at the textual level. Postcolonial critics recognize that the Bible itself contains colonial ideologies that need to be neutralized and transformed. Postcolonial critics see both the emancipating and enervating character of the biblical texts. "Postcolonialism is more guarded in its approach to Bible's serviceability. It sees the Bible as both a safe and an unsafe text, and as both a familiar and a distant one."[2]

With regard to the discipline of biblical interpretations, Fernando Segovia calls our attention to an ongoing transformation in the way the scripture is read theologically. He tries to map out the movement of the discipline of the theological reading of the Bible from a historicized to a modulated historicized reading. Biblical critics began to realize that the historicized theological reading, mediated by historical criticism, became the dominant model in the theological reading of the Bible. However, historical criticism does not consider the text as it appears despite the fact that the text per se is worthy of analysis. Segovia also stresses the importance of context and its corresponding sociocultural features in the theological reading of the Bible. Hence, the biblical critics began to modulate the historicized theological reading of the Bible through literary criticism and sociocultural criticism.

Further, Segovia provides a sketch for the fourth model of interpretation which he called ideological criticism. He highlights the role of the reader. "A number of voices began to argue that behind all recreations of meaning and reconstructions of history, behind all methods and models, stood real readers and that such flesh-and-blood readers were always and inescapably contextualized and perspectival."[3]

Under the second model of interpretation (literary criticism) among the models which Segovia has mapped out, structuralist criticism emerged as a tool of analysis. This tool focuses on the network of relationships between textual elements from which the textual meaning is constructed. But with the advent of poststructuralism, the focus shifted to the relationship between texts. Jacques Derrida, for example, claims: "There is nothing outside of the text."[4] Thus, intertextuality is employed to see the complex relationship existing between texts.

Intertextuality was first used by the post-structuralist theorists. "The term intertextuality was initially employed by post-structuralist theorists and critics in their attempt to disrupt notions of stable meaning and objective interpretation."[5] Although the term and concept originated in the field of literary theory, the complexity of intertextuality as a term and a concept presents itself to be true also to intertextual reading of biblical texts. In its application to biblical studies, intertextuality is commonly viewed as mere scriptural citations of one scriptural text by another.

One first needs to understand the distinction between the two orientations with regard to intertextuality. Geoffrey Miller offers a review of literature on intertextuality for the past two decades of Old Testament study, highlighting the two different orientations concerning intertextuality: the author-oriented approach and the reader-oriented approach.[6]

The author-oriented approach is diachronic while the reader-oriented approach is synchronic in nature. The similarity in terms of vocabulary and phraseology is suggestive of an approach in intertextuality that is diachronic. In an author-oriented intertextual approach, the authorial intent is being primarily considered and the focus is on tracing out the influence of an earlier text to a later text through the use of either quotation, allusion or echo. In a reader-oriented intertextual approach, the authorial intent is set aside for the reader to give the meaning of the text.

Julia Kristeva is the one who coined the term and one of those who first systematically developed the concept of intertextuality. In this idea of intertextuality, the reader takes an active role in the neutralization of meaning existing between texts. "It also means close scrutiny of the roles readers–especially critical readers–play in perpetuating these systems, as subjective agents engaged in the violent acts of neutralization.[7] As originally conceived, intertextuality is not about source-finding but transformation. Kristeva, following the idea of Mikhail Bakhtin, affirms the mosaic character of every text, claiming that "any text is constructed as a mosaic of quotations; any text is the absorption and transformation of another."[8] Therefore, the reader-oriented intertextuality, as an approach, is closer to Kristeva's idea.

II. Differentiation: God's Gift to Creation

This paper is a reader-oriented intertextual reading of Genesis 1:1–2:3 and Job 29:1-25. This reading concurs with Robert Alter's observation with regard to the narrative development of metaphor (narrativity) in biblical poetry that has a beginning, a development and a climax. Narrativity is also found in a narrative or prose.[9]

Our reading of Genesis 1:1–2:3 through the key-words "light" (*'ōr*) and "darkness" (*chōshek*) appearing in Genesis 1:1-5 gives us the metaphor of separation as God's way of empowering hiscreation to thrive. The textual context of Genesis 1:1–2:3 shows that the language of separation is profoundly tied up with the entire creation process. The thematic idea is that God created everything (Gen 1:1).[10] After this thematic idea, the narrativity begins in Genesis 1:2, which narrates the pre-separation condition. Verse 3 marks the start of the development of the narrativity. Ambiguous as it may be, our textual evidence tells of the existence of the darkness prior to the creation of the light. The reader can only take it from the thematic idea that the creation of the heavens and the earth includes the creation of the darkness and the deep. Verse 2 gives us the impression about the Spirit of God hovering over the face of the waters while seemingly watching over the darkness upon the face of the deep. This condition is broken when God created the light (Gen 1:3); and upon seeing thc light to be good, God separated the light from the darkness (Gen 1:4). God, it seems to me, has empowered the darkness upon the creation of the light. Moreover, God gave to the light and the darkness their respective names (Gen 1:5a), implying that God has no intention of eradicating the darkness. And immediately, the rotation of evening and morning happened for the first time, which has set the beginning of days and seasons.

This narrativity continued to develop until it has reached its climax when everything has already been created and that the last in the list, human beings, are mandated to be fruitful and multiply, to fill the earth and subdue it. The verb "to subdue" could metaphorically refer to the imperative of standing against any absolute independence in favor of interdependence. Human beings are also given the imperative "to rule over" or "to thrive together with" the fish of the sea, the birds of the air and all the living things moving on the earth. This is the climax of the narrativity of a narrative that ends with the creator-God resting in order to allow to creation to thrive interdependently.

The narrativity that we have seen in Genesis 1:1–2:3 presents creation as an ongoing process. Creation is not over yet. Creation is empowered by the creator-God to thrive. Separation is necessary if creatures are to thrive because thriving happens when there is differentiation in view of an interdependent relationship.[11] In line with the metaphor of "light" and "darkness," what is being conveyed is that the darkness is needed as much as the light is also needed for creation to flourish. Darkness is not something to be eradicated. Even if it is a common knowledge that Genesis 1:1–2:3 or 1:1–2:4 comes from the Priestly Tradition (P creation narrative), with its central idea of separation, this creation narrative cannot be fully understood through a mere binary logic. Separation must lead to interdependence and not to isolation and domination.

The idea of an unfinished creation, in line with the metaphor of "light" and "darkness," becomes even more dramatic in the face of suffering. With this, Genesis 1:1–2:3 is intertextually linked with Job 29:1-25. Our reading of Job 29:1-25, through the key-words "light" and "darkness," found in Job 29:2-6, gives us the thematic idea expressed in the poetic lines: "when his lamp shone upon my head, // and by his light I walked through the darkness" (Job 29:3). The thematic idea here tells of Job as the center around which everything revolves. In Job 29:1-25, the narrativity begins also in verse 3. The change of geographical location is clearly marked in this poetic text. In Job 29:2-6, the readers are inside Job's tent. Everything within this tent revolves around Job.

The narrativity accelerates in Job 29:7 when the location shifts to the city gate where everyone else listens to Job while he performs his social obligations. This narrativity will continue to develop until Job 29:24 wherein no one is able to cast down the "light" of Job's countenance or face (cf. "my face"). The narrativity reaches its climax in Job 29:25 when Job becomes the chief and dwells like a king among his troops. The entire poetic unit, except Job 29:2a, places Job at the center of everything. Job 29:2a, right away, gives an idea to the readers that the good things Job enumerated remain only in Job's recollection of his past life. Job's reality is filled with suffering and he tends to associate these sufferings with the darkness. Moreover, the metaphor of "light" and "darkness" (cf. Jb 29:3, 24) plays an important role in the narrativity found in this poetic unit of Job 29:1-25. The words "light" and "darkness" both appear in Job 29:3 while only the word "light" occurs in Job 29:24. In Job's mind, at least in his recollection, darkness seemed to be no more when no one was able to cast down the light of his face (Jb 29:24).

This metaphor of "light" and "darkness" manifests a network of connections elsewhere in the Book of Job. "Light" becomes a metaphor for a perfect creation while "darkness" becomes a metaphor for creation's imperfections. Job does not really know this realm of "light" and "darkness" that he finds it difficult to accept the fact that they co-exist in creation. Job could not also reconcile how an omnipotent God would create a creation with such flaws. In addition, since Job cannot eradicate darkness, he now operates in the binary logic of retribution, upon which he could simply set aside the love for life in the name of retributive justice. Since he cannot eradicate the experience of imperfections (i.e.), he now wants to eradicate everything. Job begins seeing God as an enemy. He now prefers an absolute independence. Job wants to set aside his oneness with the creator-God as well as with the rest of creation because he could not come into terms with the fact that "light" and "darkness" coexist interdependently in an already empowered creation. Nevertheless, God's offer to Job is partnership. "Rather, God is a partner in the struggle against forces that impede the (originally intended) perfection of the universe."[12]

Both Genesis 1:1–2:3 and Job 29:1-25, with the key-words "light" and "darkness," show that creation remains to be an ongoing process. Our reading of these two biblical texts, appearing to be in dialogue with each other, has also shown that the entire creation is empowered by the creator-God so that life may flourish. This thriving of life will only happen when the process of differentiation is recognized as something oriented towards interdependence and not towards isolation and domination.

Being created by the creator-God is a gift. Likewise, being empowered by the same God through differentiation is also a gift. The empowerment of human beings through differentiation is further qualified in the creation of human beings – they are created in God's own image and likeness. This kind of differentiation is intricately tied up with a certain task which is to be in solidarity with the creator-God and with creation.

III. Solidarity with God and Creation: A Human Task

There seems to me a kind of buildup concerning this differentiation of creatures that reaches its climax in the creation of human being (*'ādām*), with whom the creator-God, despite the clear differentiation between the creator and creatures, exhibits a kind of closer relation. "Then God said, 'Let us make man in our image, after our likeness…" (Gen 1:26a). This is followed by another description of differentiation which is intertwined with the creation of *'ādām*. This oneness despite differentiation is well expressed in Genesis 1:27: "So God created man in his own image, in the image of God he created him; male and female he created them." One *'ādām* (humanity) is created. God created them "male" *(zākār)* and "female" (*neqebāh)*. This verse expresses God's oneness with human beings despite the clear differentiation, and the oneness of human beings with one another despite their differentiation. Furthermore, the triple use of the verb "to create" (*bārā'*) in this verse presents itself purposefully supporting the idea of oneness amidst differentiation.

Profoundly connected to the thematic idea about God creating everything is the idea of oneness. God created the heavens and the earth and all that they contain, and all of these created realities, in their varieties express oneness with the creator-God and with one another. Moreover, God himself empowers all created realities.

In as far as human beings are concerned, the set of imperatives: be fruitful, multiply, fill and subdue the earth (Gen 1:28) may also be related to this narrativity of oneness despite differentiation. In the narrative, the reader may recall that the earth is the first one to have been empowered (Gen 1:12), but this empowerment seems to have the need to be regulated and neutralized in Genesis 1:24 by God himself. Now, in Genesis 1:28, it appears that the mandate to human beings to subdue the earth functions to mandate human beings to be in solidarity with the creator-God in regulating and neutralizing any tendency of anything within the created order towards an absolute independence. This summons for human beings to be in solidarity with the creator-God is to keep the value of interdependence which is needed in the flourishing of life in an ongoing creation process.

In the language of retribution found in the Book of Job, the light and the darkness, can be, and must be, separated categorically. Otherwise "the chief" who sees himself as the center of everything, if given the power, would be wanting to eradicate darkness, and if not, to eradicate the light as expressed in the poetic lines: "Let that day be darkness! // May God above not seek it, // nor light shine upon it" (Job 3:4). The immediate textual context of Job 3:4 expresses an anti-creation sentiment akin to the desire of annihilating whatever is perceived to be not within the ambit of light such as Job's very existence that has been darkened by the experience of suffering: "Let the day perish when I was born, // and the night which said, 'a man-child is conceived" (Job 3:3). God is the creator of both "light" and "darkness" and not of "light" alone. Further, creation burst when YHWH prescribed bounds for thick darkness (Job 38:10). Creation is not yet finished and Job is invited to do his part in this ongoing perfection of creation. It does not matter if Job's trust in God's omnipotence is what seems to be at stake. What matters most is that God loves his creation and that he cares for it, getting himself involved in an ongoing process of perfecting the created world.

Oneness with the creator-God is oneness with the rest of creation because God cares for his creation. Job is invited to exercise solidarity with the creator-God in allowing life to flourish. Job is also invited to be in solidarity with an already empowered creation moving towards its perfection.

IV. Conclusion

A reader-oriented intertextual reading of Genesis 1:1–2:3 and Job 29:1-25 has shown the intricate relationship between light and darkness, differentiated as they are. The dominant interpretation that the light is good and that the darkness is bad, and that the darkness needs to be eradicated, is put under an exegetical suspicion. Now, the meaning of the relationship existing between them is neutralized and transformed. Light and darkness are both needed for creation to thrive and for life to flourish.

The narrativity of light and darkness, generated by our intertextual reading of Genesis 1:1–2:3 and Job 29:1-25, has exposed the dominant meaning in the understanding of the relationship between light and darkness. The dominant interpretation carries with it an ideology that marginalizes and eradicate the differently other. This dominant meaning must shift to an understanding that values interdependence.

Human beings, created in the image and likeness of God, are empowered to regulate and neutralize any tendency towards absolute independence in view of interdependence. Hence, human empowerment per se is neither for isolation nor domination. They are differentiated from God, but with this particular task, they are also in one with God. Moreover, with this particular task, human beings are also differentiated from other creatures. However, as being empowered by God for the flourishing of life, they are also in one with the rest of created realities. Therefore, it is a human task to be in solidarity with the creator-God and with creation, so that the entire created order may thrive and life may flourish through an interdependent relationship.

Notes

1. See Laudato Si'. See also Querida Amazonia.
2. Rasia S. Sugirtharajah, The Bible and the Third World (Cambridge: Cambridge University Press, 2004), 259.
3. Fernando F. Segovia, "A Theological Reading of Scripture? Critical Problematic and Prophetic Vision in the Aftermath and Crossroads of Disciplinary Transformation," CTSA Proceedings 65 (2010), 1-18, here 9.
4. Jacques Derrida, Of Grammatology, translated from French by Gayatri Chakravorty Spivak, corrected edition (Baltimore, Maryland: The John Hopkins University Press, 1997), 158.

5. Graham Allen, Intertextuality, The New Critical Idiom, edited by John Drakakis (London: Routledge, 2000), 3.
6. See Geoffrey G. Miller, "Intertextuality in Old Testament Research," CBR 9/3 (2010): 283-309. Miller points out the lack of certain consensus with regard to the exact nature of intertextuality.
7. George Aichele and Gary A. Phillips, "Introduction: Exegesis, Eisegesis, Intergesis," in Intertextuality and the Bible, Semeia 69.70 (1995), 7-18, here 11.
8. Julia Kristeva, Desire in Language: A Semiotic Approach to Literature and Art, translated from French and edited by Thomas Gora, Alice Jardine, Leon S. Roudiez and edited by Roudiez (New York: Columbia University Press, 1980), 66.
9. See Robert Alter, The Art of Biblical Poetry (New York: Basic Books, 1985), 27-61. See also Alter, The Art of Biblical Narrative (New York: Basic Books, 1981), 88-113.
10. See Cristino R. Pine, Living Word on Breathing Earth: Biblical Insights and Reflections on Creation (Quezon City: Claretian Communications Foundation, Inc., 2018), 11.
11. It is a common knowledge that the first account of creation (Gen. 1:1–2,3 or 1:1–2,4) comes from the Priestly Tradition (P). See Mark S. Smith, The Priestly Vision of Genesis 1 (Minneapolis: Fortress Press, 2010). Smith also registers observation similar to what we have textually observed like the term and idea of separation that is attributed to the P. See also Ska, Introduction to Reading the Pentateuch (Winona Lake, Indiana: Eisenbrauns, 2006), 187-191. Ska discusses that the Priestly Tradition provided hope for the people after the so-called Sinai covenant failed due to the unfaithfulness of the people. The people of Israel then, for the P, becomes a kind of religious assembly that has been separated. The divine presence is basically bestowed upon the priests. Ska also points out that the Holy Code, after the exile, tried to correct the Priestly Writer in several aspects of its theology. For example, the divine presence is bestowed not only upon the priests but it is something shared by all the people. The emphasis of the separation shifted to Israel being set apart from other nations.
12. André Lococque, "The Deconstruction of Job's Fundamentalism," JBL 126.1 (2007), 83-97, here 96.

Ecclesial Unity and Diversity from the Amazon synod

Víctor Codina

The Amazon Synod has caused a series of tensions in society and in the Church. Ecclesial tensions form part of the polarity that runs through its entire history between unity and diversity, between centralization and dispersion, between the universal catholic church and local churches. The overcoming of these theological and pastoral tensions is illuminated from an ecclesial synodality and an update of pneumatology.

Proem

Although one could begin to treat this issue from theoretical philosophical and theological principles, in a systematic and scientific way, I prefer to do it from below, in a kind of historical and symbolic narrative theology because "reality is more important than the idea" (EG 231-233).

Specifically, I will start from my experience of the Amazon Synod held in Rome from October 6 to 27, 2019, under the slogan "Amazon: new paths for the Church and for an integral ecology".

I. A new methodology

Already in the two preceding synods on the family and on youth, there was consultation with the grassroots, however, in the Amazon Synod the survey that the REPAM (Pan-amazonic Ecclesial Network) carried out within the Amazonian communities was very broad and its results were the basis for the elaboration of the *Instrumentum laboris* presented to the Synod Fathers as a point of reference for all their Synod contributions. Added to this was the fact that during the trip that Francis made to Puerto

Maldonado (Peru) on January 19, 2018 to meet with groups of Amazonian indigenous people, he told them that more than talking to them, above all he wanted to listen to them. The Synod has been above all a listening to the Amazonian peoples, who have become its real protagonists.

What emerges from this REPAM survey? That the Amazon is one of the richest places on the planet in flora, fauna, and water, very important for the climate balance of America and the world, but that it is now threatened and mortally wounded by the savage exploitation of multinationals in mining, oil, forestry, hydroelectricity, agrochemicals, etc., that break into their forests and jungles, pollute their rivers, endanger the lives of indigenous people who have to emigrate to the outskirts of large cities such as Manaus or Leticia, where they live at the margins, at risk of falling into drug trafficking, prostitution, and suicide of youth. Many of the leaders who protest against these injustices are eliminated and killed with impunity.

Although these peoples are economically poor, they feel they have an ancestral wisdom, prior to Christianity. Their ideal of "living well", that is to say, in harmony with the community, with nature, and with the Divine, is a great wealth and an alternative to the modern style that seeks an always better life at the expense of others and the earth.

To the Church, they lament their colonialist past and ask for an ecclesial presence of missionaries, not visiting, but permanent and inculturated, and the possibility that married and mature indigenous people can be ordained as priests. That the fundamental role of women in pastoral care be recognized and that the female diaconate be considered.

The presence of indigenous men and women among the group of theological experts (Justino Sarmiento, Eleazar López, Patricia Gualinga…) and that others also had access to the floor at the Synod was a novelty.

This indigenous presence profoundly marked the entire synodal process, with highly realistic and prophetic interventions: that the Church defend them from multinationals and businesses that threaten them with death; that the bishops meditate on the gospel of the final judgment (Matthew 25); that the bishops support the Pope who is alone and row alongside him; that the mission of the nuns who baptize, celebrate the Word, marry, burry, and "confess" be valued; that they do not consider climate change as a secondary problem, because for indigenous people it is a matter of life and death, etc.

Also indigenous and other collaborators, theologians, religious and lay people made up the group called "Common Home" who participated in some Vatican ceremonies, such as the inaugural procession of the Synod, on October 7, from Saint Peter to the Synod room, with songs, dances, and colourful symbols, carrying nets, a boat, and some images of a pregnant woman that represented the fertility of Mother Earth.

II. Critical reactions

Social Media, from the beginning to the end of the synodal stage, focused on two ecclesiastical themes of the Synod: the ordination of viri probati and the female diaconate, silencing the ecological and planetary dimension of the Synod. Is this silence of the Media on ecology and on the Synod's prophetic criticism of multinationals and governments by chance? Is today's society really very interested in the frequent Eucharistic participation of indigenous peoples?

The *Instrumentum laboris* was criticized by high ecclesial dignitaries: pantheistic, denying universal salvation in Christ, mythologizing the natives, and concealing their ancient human sacrifices, a stupid text, which wanted us to return to the caves, to bows and arrows, it defended a biodegradable ecology. The procession to the Synod room, by the Pope, bishops, synod members, and indigenous in a festive atmosphere and in the midst of a beautiful disorder, was described as the Rio Carnival, and the images of pregnant women that symbolized the fertility of the Earth were later through into the Tiber by some hotheads, who claimed that they were idols.

While the synodal contributions of the Amazonian bishops reflected their closeness as pastors to a suffering and believing people, and a majority understood their pastoral proposals, the contributions of bishops from other places and of curial dignitaries, with some notable exceptions, were rather reticent and critical of pastoral changes; they defended the unity and tradition of the Church, avoiding divisions and dangerous new developments; some even defended an almost ontological and essential relationship between celibacy and priestly ministry.

In spite of everything, the Synod's proposals were all approved by

2/3: a Church with an Amazonian face, creation of an Amazonian rite, ordination of married indigenous people and with families, advance on the issue of the female diaconate, the creation of a kind of Amazonian Episcopal Conference to concretize the Synod pastorally, etc.

The Post-Synodal Exhortation *Querida Amazonía* also provoked criticism, both from conservative sectors of the Church and from progressive groups who expected otherwise from Francis' post-synodal document, surely more concerned with their own theological views than with Amazonian indigenous people, who received the document with great joy and satisfaction.

On June 29, 2020, the Pope constituted not an Amazonian Episcopal Organism but the Ecclesial Conference of the Amazon, in collaboration with CELAM, but with its own autonomy. Not only are representatives of the seven Amazonian Episcopal Conferences part of it, but Liliana Franco representing the Latin American Conference of Religious, a representative of Caritas, and of REPAM, and three members of the Amazonian indigenous peoples: Patricia Gualinga, Laura Vicuña y Delio Siticonantzi. The importance of this Amazonian Ecclesial Conference not only affects the local Amazonian church but also opens paths for the future beyond the existing Episcopal conferences. It is the first ecclesial fruit of the Synod and a new opening to synodality.

Undoubtedly, in this synodal process we are faced with two difference ecclesiologies, an ecclesiology that puts unity before diversity and defends a uniform centralism, at its base patriarchal and clerical, and another ecclesiology that has a different vision of the Church, a communion of local Churches, with greater respect for the plurality of places, cultures, and times, a multifaceted Church that does not identify or confuse unity with uniformity, or progress with a breakdown of tradition. The Amazon Synod has produced not only an ecclesial confrontation, but has revealed once again the permanent ecclesial tension between unity and diversity. This deserves to be addressed.

III. The three ecclesiological millennia

In ecclesiology, the historical existence of three different millennia is commonly admitted, with the caveat that they are not chronological but ecclesiological millennia, sometimes behind and sometimes ahead of calendar dates.

III.i. The first ecclesiological millennium

This encompasses the Church of the first centuries, the passage from the apostolic to the post-apostolic and patristic Church, deeply marked by the Constantinian turn, but whose spirit of openness to a Church as mystery of communion and many of its structures survive until the 11th century. It is a Church close to its origins, persecuted for centuries that maintains unity and communion in the midst of great geographical and cultural diversity, celebrates regional synods, with a Petrine Primate, who wants to be a servant of the servants of God. Undoubtedly, we run the risk of idealizing this and forgetting its heresies, tensions in the ecumenical councils, and the sins of a chaste and prostitute, holy and sinful Church. This ecclesiology is experiential and implicit, symbolic and liturgical rather than systematic. The presence of the Spirit is manifested strongly in all the People of God.

III.ii. The second millennium

Lasting until Vatican II, it covers the so-called Christendom, which begins with Gregory VII, who, to defend ecclesial freedom against secular princes, centralizes and standardizes ecclesial structures. There is a deep liturgical and sacramental evolution, the Petrine primacy is called the Vicar of Christ, there is an "ecclesial papalization" (J. O'Malley), and a weakening of all local structures. Signs of ecclesian opposition emerge such as monasticism in the 4th century, the separation in the 11th century between Rome and the Eastern Church of Constantinople, the emergence of lay movements from the 11th to 13th centuries, and the desire for a true evangelical reform in the 16th century with very diverse results: the Churches of the Protestant Reformation and a Catholic renewal, with Trent and the emergence of contemplative and apostolic religious movements. Again, the tension between unity and diversity and the local Churches and Rome appears. The first scientific ecclesiologies appear in the fourteenth century as theological treatises on the power of the Pope against secular royal power. Once again, it is the triumph of uniform clericalism over regional and lay diversity. The peak of the ecclesial hierarchy occurs at the First Vatican Council, where the primacy of the Roman Pontiff and his infallibility are proclaimed when he speaks ex cathedra. The ecclesiology of the local Churches disappears.

Also here, we cannot be too strongly negative, because despite this, the Church grew, evangelized continents, maintained the faith of the people; holiness and a multitude of charisms flourished, fruit of the Spirit.

III.iii. The third millennium

This millennium begins with John XXIII and the Second Vatican Council (1962-1965). There is a change in the ecclesial model: it moves from a clerical Church to a Church of the People of God, a people of the baptized (LG II); from a triumphalist Church to a Church serving humanity (GS 40-43) that follows the path of the poor Jesus (LG 48) towards eschatology (LG VII); from a juridical Church , to a mystery and sacrament Church that is born of the Trinity (LG 1), animated by the Spirit (LG 4), and reflects the light of Christ (LG 1).

One of the novelties was the issue of episcopal collegiality (LG 22), which without denying what was affirmed by Vatican I about the Roman pontiff, who is the one who presides over the episcopal college, complements and balances it from a more communal dimension and with a universal co-responsibility both in the magisterium and in the pastoral. Along with this, the notion of the local Church reappears, the greatest ecclesiological novelty according to Karl Rahner: the local or particular Churches are not a part of the universal Church, but a portion of the universal Church (CD 1); the particular Churches, of which each bishop is the start and foundation of unity, are formed in the image of the universal Church and in them and from them, the one and only universal Church is formed (LG 23).

The ecclesiology of the third millennium recovers the essential community elements of the Church of the first millennium, and opens itself to dialogue with the contemporary world, alongside which it is walking towards the Kingdom. It is not about the Church and the world today, but about the Church in the world today.

III.iv. The Post-Council

The aggiornamento engendered by Vatican II, produced exaggerations in some ecclesial sectors and in other groups, reactions of a conservative type, symbolized by Bishop Marcel Lefèbvre who in the council led the conservative minority and later, rejected the council because he considered it neo-Protestant and neo-Modernist.

Already during Vatican II, in view of the fear of a possible ecclesial schism, a *Nota praevia* was introduced, by higher order, at the end of *Lumen Gentium*, in which the primacy of the Pope as head of the episcopal college was reaffirmed in such a way that collegiality becomes something discretionary, free, prudential, non-binding, with which the risk of returning to the situation of Vatican I begins. Paul VI signs the conciliar documents, not as bishop of Rome, but as "bishop of the Universal Church."

A process of conciliar regression begins that led to the ecclesial winter of the pontificates of John Paul II and Benedict XVI. Universality once again suffocates the local Churches. The reactions against the Amazon Synod have a distant origin. Let us list some of the main links in this increasing retreat to Christendom.

Paul VI acted in a very personal and non-collegial way in the encyclicals *Sacerdotalis coelibatus y Humanae vitae* (1968), creating a lot of tension in various ecclesial sectors, as well as in the 1976 decree, *Inter insigniores* against female ordination.

This was aggravated by John Paul II. *The Code of Canon Law* (1983) favors a centralist vision of the hierarchical Church. The Synod of 1985, convened for an evaluation of Vatican II, although it offers a positive vision of the Council, substitutes the concept of 'the People of God' Church with 'the Body of Christ' Church. As Cardinal Josef Ratzinger is the Prefect of the Congregation of the Doctrine of the Faith, the decree *Communionis notio* (1992) asserts that the universal Church is a reality ontologically and chronologically prior to the local Church, thereby breaking the equilibrium of *Lumen Gentium*. Faced with this assertion, Walter Kasper and Carlos María Martini reacted against it. Also in 1992, the *Catechism of the Catholic Church* was published, a proposal that at Vatican II had been rejected by the bishops. In 1998, the decree, *Apostolos suos*, restricted the doctrinal power of the Episcopal Conferences. The two Instructions against the Latin American theology of liberation (1984 and 1986) and the censorship of some of its theologians, shows once again the incapacity of understanding the dialogue between Rome and the local churches. John Paul II in *Ordinatio sacerdotalis*, 1994, rejects the priestly ordination of women as something that must be considered by the faithful of the Church as "definitive." He did not have to wait long for critical reactions, not only from women but also from theologians due to the risk of identifying "definitive" with "infallible." John Paul II perceived the seriousness of these problems and in his ecumenical encyclical *Ut unum sint* (1995), he asks the Christian Churches and their theologians for help to rethink together the exercise of the primacy of Peter (95-95).

The pontificate of Benedict XVI follows the theological line of John Paul II, of which he himself had been the promoter, insisting on the continuity of Vatican II with Tradition rather than on its novelty. The admirable and exemplary resignation of Benedict XVI was not only due to problems of age and health, but to the failure of his attempt to eliminate relativism and ecclesial tensions. He felt the anguish in the nave of a Church in the middle of a storm while Jesus slept.

IV. Synodality

When the new Pope Francis introduced himself to the Church and to the world as Bishop of Rome, many perceived that something was changing in the Church. The symbolic gestures of Francis with children, the sick, and the elderly, his graphic expressions of the Church going out to the peripheries, the field hospital, smelling the sheep, the poor Church and the poor, the polyhedral Church, etc., they could lead to the conclusion that Francis is a pastoral Pope without a serious theological foundation or path. His various documents such as *Evangelii gaudium, Laudato si, Amoris laetitia, Querida Amazonía,* etc., show us that there is not theological or pastoral improvisation. This appears clearly when Francis begins to address the topic of synodality on October 16, 2015 in the synod of the family, with a speech of great theological depth. The International Theological Commission, after four years of work, published on May 3, 2018 the document *Synodality in the Life and Mission of the Church.* Francis, on September 15, 2018, published the *Constitution Episcopalis communio.*

The term synodality is spontaneously associated with a meeting or synod of bishops, but in reality synodality is something much broader; it is a constitutive dimension of the Church. John Chrysostom affirms that "synod is the name of the Church."[1] Etymologically, synod means "joint (*syn*) path (*hodos*)", that is, a path travelled with others, where both the dimension of fraternity and communion and the historical dynamism of walking together towards the Kingdom of God are accentuated, under the strength of the Spirit. Synodality is an expression of the ecclesiology of communion, of the *koinonía* of all the baptized who walk in history toward eschatological fullness. The Church is a synodal Church, although this term has over time been reduced to episcopal synods. If we evoke the term synodality here, it is because it offers us a fundamental theological key to harmoniously integrate the tension between ecclesial unity and diversity.

Let us present some of the main lines of these documents:

Synodality springs from the Trinitarian community of God, where unity and plurality are harmonized in a mysterious communion of interpersonal love, which overflows outwards in the Father's creative and loving project of constituting a united people, living in communion with God, interhuman and cosmic community, through Christ and in the Spirit, of which the one, holy, catholic, and apostolic Church is a sacrament (LG 1; AG 2-4) and the Eucharist its liturgical paschal expression.

The entire Old Testament is oriented toward the constitution of this People of God, whose ultimate meaning does not appear until Jesus of Nazareth, his paschal mystery, and the gift of the Spirit that is communicated to us through baptism; the *sensus fidelium* makes the holy people infallible in their faith (LG 12).

This requires that the Church be participatory and dialogical, in intimate communion of pastors and faithful, a Church that is always teaching and learning, where pastors listen to their faithful to know what the Spirit says to the Church, and the faithful follow their pastors as custodians and interpreters of the ecclesial faith. The synodal Church is a *communio fidelium, communio episcoporum, y communio ecclesiarum.*

This synodality that was already expressed in the so-called Council of Jerusalem (Acts 15; Gal 2), was kept alive in the first millennium, declines in the second western ecclesial millennium with a weakening of the local Churches and great internal ruptures of the Church. It was not until Vatican II that the basic theological elements of synodality reappeared (*Lumen Gentium y Christus Dominus*).

Synodality has ecumenical implications for inter-church dialogue and also for dialogue with society, with which the Church walks together towards the fullness of the Kingdom. Hence the importance of discerning the signs of the times to listen to what the Spirit tells us today (GS 4; 11; 44). For Francis, synodality is the path that God expects from the Church of the third millennium.

Synodality breaks with all ecclesial clericalism, grants the laity and other communities a leading role in the Church, in a climate of continuous dialogue, consultation, and listening. Hence the importance of dialogue between the universal Church and local Churches, intercultural and interreligious dialogue, the dialogue between universality and geographical, historical, cultural, and religious particularities.

In this synodal journey between the Churches and the creeds, there must be a special solidarity with the poorest and most excluded members of society, and listen to their voice, since they constitute a true theological locus (EG 126)

Synodality today also has ecological repercussions since we are all part of the same common home and we walk together with all creation to eschatological fullness; the earth wishes to be freed from the birth pains that it now suffers (Rm 8, 20-22) and overcome the anthropocentric and technocratic paradigm that destroys creation (*Laudato sí*).

Let us say finally that synodality and Pneumatology are so closely connected that when Pneumatology is obscured, ecclesial synodality is obscured. The Spirit is always acting in the Church and in society, a Spirit of universality and pluralism as revealed at Pentecost, contrary to Babel, which is the idolatry of an exclusive uniformity. And the Spirit ordinarily acts from below, from the poor, *de profundis* of history.

V. Return to the Synod

The tensions of the Synod are born from the tension between a uniform abstract universality and the plurality of the poor Amazonian peoples and their local Churches with their own geography, culture, religion, language, and history. For some, this Synod has been a disaster, as it has not responded to plans drawn up from offices; for others, it has been magnificent. Since it has listened to the cry of the poor and indigenous, it has been an exercise in synodality.

Both conservatives and progressives expected from *Querida Amazonía* a definitive papal position on ecclesial issues, but Francis surely preferred that unity prevail over conflict (EG 226-230), a unity that is the fruit of synodal discernment and an overflow of the Spirit, not an imposition from above. The road is longer but more fruitful. The main actor of the Synod has been the Spirit, who acts from below; it is always puzzling and new. The next Synod will be on synodality.

The statues of pregnant women thrown into the Tiber can symbolize that in this Synod, the Amazon plunged into Rome and Rome opened itself to the world. Church and society began to Amazonize themselves.

Translated by Thia Cooper

Note

1.Exp in Psalm 149,1; PG 55, 493

Part Four: Response to the Issue

Incarnation, Territoriality, and New Pastoral Paths: the Itinerary of REPAM and the Amazon Synod

Mauricio López Oropeza

The Amazon Synod, a milestone in recent ecclesiology, has its origin in an experience of territorial pastoral praxis that found its point of great development with the Pan-Amazonian Ecclesial Network (REPAM). This network is the result of the embodied experience of church members in this territory, who through light and shadow, have helped to outline inculturated and intercultural pastoral perspectives, shaping an Amazonian face for the Church. At the juncture of the Synod and its connection with Laudato Si', new paths are opened to respond to the most urgent challenges of the territory, and as a paradigm for a pastoral reflection of the whole Church.

> *"La esencia de la Iglesia está en su misión de servicio al mundo,*
> *En su misión de salvarlo en totalidad y de salvarlo en la historia, aquí y ahora.*
> *La Iglesia está para solidarizarse con las esperanzas y los gozos,*
> *con las angustias y tristezas de los hombres".*
> ("The essence of the Church in in its mission of service to the world,
> In its mission of saving the world in its totality and of saving it in history, here and now.
> The Church is to be in solidarity with the hopes and joys,
> with the anguish and sorrows, of men.")
> *San Óscar A. Romero. Discurso en Lovaina, 1980*

I. Territoriality as a space for the incarnation and for new pastoral paths

Reality(ies) is/are the sum of existential phenomena in permanent transformation, in transition, and above all processes that are (and by us) constructed, deconstructed, and reconstructed, based on the interactions between social subjects, and with the contexts in which we exist and on which we depend. The human being, with all its dimensions and grey areas, is the preponderant axis to understand this/these reality/ies from a rationality that is a gift and a challenge, and as something always unfinished. But it is not about an autonomous social subject, but one that is recognized in its multidimensional identity considering the anthropological, social, cultural, political, spiritual, ecological, and economic spheres.

We are the result of our history, of cultural references, formative processes, symbolic experiences (even of religious phenomena), and of the geographical space where we have lived with its circumstances and accents; and, above all, we are the result of our decisions regarding our relationship with other human beings and our environment. This, as a whole, accounts for a *territoriality* that reflects how: "The social world is accumulated history, and… it is not to be reduced to a discontinuous series of instantaneous mechanical equilibria between agents who are treated as interchangeable particles."[1]

Territoriality, as a social and symbolic construction, must be assumed from a complex network of relationships of inter-knowledge, inter-recognition, and inter-dependence, since *everything is connected*.[2] This is true, also, for those apparently intangible aspects such as our culture and spirituality, and the relationships with the natural environment of which we are part, which determines the possibility of our existence. We are and exist in relation to *the other*, but above all with the other subjects with whom we share this life.

For many native cultures, as is the case for so many that inhabit the Amazon, the territory means a relationship with their spirituality, with their origin and identities, and with the land, spirits, and species with whom they co-habit, and who they co-depend on in existential reciprocity.

The Spiritual Exercises of Saint Ignatius, a substantial element of Ignatian spirituality and patrimony of the Church, allow us to contemplate and drink in the depths of the creative mystery of God. This opens us to new epistemologies that can connect with this territorial dimension that is essential in theological-pastoral reflection for the field of ecclesial mission. We are invited to insert ourselves into the very experience of a loving father-mother God, and contemplate the very moment of the act of God's territorialisation, the Incarnation.

For believers, follows of a living Christ, redeemer of reality, the Incarnation is a real event that continues to take place in our midst and in front of our eyes, especially in those places considered "peripheral". The birth of Christ in the margins reflects a material and existential choice of God, and of God's life project yearned for by all humanity. The contemplation of the Incarnation allows us a unique understanding of the inter-connection that sustains all relationships in a specific territoriality:

> This will be to listen to what the persons on the face of the earth say, that is, how they speak to one another… I will also hear what the Divine Persons say, that is, "Let us work the redemption of the human race"(…) namely, work the most holy incarnation.[3]

It is through the Incarnation that we are given a new understanding as believers, which allows us to build different relationships with everything that is created. In this act of redemption we also recognize the ecological dimension of territoriality. Which, in the Incarnation, is understaood as the fruit of the creative-creator will of God as an expression of God's "love" for all that is created and towards all God's creatures.

In the keys to our contemporary territorial pastoral care, the Second Vatican Council called upon all the domestic churches to insert themselves into cultures *"in harmony with the economy of the Incarnation*" (AG 22). The territorial dynamics of the Incarnation occur in the cultures of the peoples themselves, and "the Church, the People of God inserted among the people of the world, has the beauty of a multiform face because it is rooted in many cultures (EG 116). Each "major socio-cultural area" (AG 22b) marks the face of a church or a group of churches. The catholicity of the one People of God is realized in the rich diversity of cultures and generates "the variety of local churches" (LG 23), with their theological, liturgical, spiritual, pastoral, and canonical particularities (LG 23d, AG 19).[4]

II. Amazonian territoriality: the horizon and a new networked pastoral path

The experience of the disciple and missionary church in the Pan-Amazonian geographic, ecosystemic, spiritual, and socio-cultural territoriality represents unprecedented ecclesial paths in the commitment to the peripheries. The ecclesial role has been, to say the least and despite its many limitations and serious errors, decisive in many ways for this territory.

The many testimonies of faith and dedication of missionary men and women, religious, laity, and priests and bishops, account for a possible pastoral experience of inculturation and interculturality that have made a difference in the lives of so many indigenous, mestizo, and riverine communities in the Amazon. They are a source of hope, amid so many undesirable examples of a dominating and overwhelming ecclesial model that is far from the desire for the Gospel, so that all peoples may have life in all its fullness.

Although the ecclesial presence has been significant in many cases, it has also been an absolutely fragmented presence in this immense territory. Today the challenge is so complex and so urgent, due to the innumerable threats against the life of the peoples and the Amazonian ecosystem, that it is essential to assume a territorial pastoral perspective. If we do not create new articulated paths, we will not have much more to do in the face of the systematic death that weights on this territory and its communities.

To remain silent, or to simply respond in deterritorialized and superficial ways, would be an act of complicity with the many who strip and tear life from the Amazon and its peoples, putting the planet's future at rish due to the interconnection of this biome and its peoples with the global equilibrium.

In this context, after several decades of multiple attempts, experiences, and territorial meetings to exchange ecclesial experiences about the Amazon, a more organic, territorial pastoral process has been triggered that articulates the diverse experiences in this socio-cultural space. This nascent process seeks to gradually weave, with limitations and challenges, an authentic pastoral of the whole.

The Pan-Amazonian Ecclesial Network (REPAM) was born in April 2013 in the Amazonian periphery of Puyo, Ecuador, to be later formalized in September 2014 in Brasilia, with the mission of strengthening the action carried out by the Catholic Church in the Amazonian territory, updating and specifying joint and comprehensive apostolic options within the framework of the doctrine and orientations of the Church. The priority subjects of REPAM's mission are the communities and indigenous peoples of the Amazon with its richness and cultural diversity, and the most vulnerable groups. Pope Francis, at the start of REPAM, challenged us to consider that:

> We cannot live alone, closed in on ourselves; we have to love and be loved, we need tenderness. Only in this way, can the Christian witness, thanks to the network, reach the human existential peripheries, allowing the Christian leaven to fertilize and enable the living cultures of the Amazon to progress.[5]

In this effort, in permanent reconfiguration, a multiplicity of pre-existing territorial ecclesial experiences have participated together with the Latin American Episcopal Council – CELAM, the Commission for the Amazon of the Episcopal Conference of Brazil – CNBB, the Latin American and Caribbean Secretariat of Cáritas, and the Latin American and Caribbean Conference of Religious- CLAR, in addition to multiple ecclesial nuclei, pastoral agents, and itinerant teams, congregations, specialized institutions, organizations of indigenous peoples, international Church networks, and the close support of various authorities of the Vatican. All of them together, in a highly unlikely scenario due to its complexity, but equally urgent due to the unsustainable situation of threats to the Amazon and its peoples, have launched an unprecedented experience of pastoral articulation in a specific territory.

Paraphrasing some of the REPAM documents, its vocation is to be a platform that allows the diverse subjects of the territory TO WALK TOGETHER with their own experiences and in unity, without intending to be uniform. To be a SERVANT that promotes and encourages concrete responses and approaches to the peripheries for their promotion. To assume a vocation of LISTENING to the people in the territory and to know their dreams, cries, and horizons, leaving the self-reference as church. To promote a missionary perspective of the church PRESENT IN THE TERRITORY, capable of inculturation and interculturation in reality.

And to assume a PROPHETIC ROLE of announcement and denunciation in the face of the signs of death that weigh on the Amazon and its peoples, receiving and sustaining the testimony of women and men, martyrs and prophets of the church and the territory.

REPAM must be understood in this historical moment as a consequence of the revelation of the Spirit in the Magisterium of the Church in Latin America in the V CELAM, in Aparecida, where they express the need to "raise awareness in the Americans about the importance of the Amazon for all humanity. To establish, among the local churches of various South American countries in the Amazon basin, a joint pastoral with differentiated priorities to create a development model that provileges the poor and serves the common good."[6]

III. The essential features of REPAM: NETWORK- ECCLESI-AL- PANAMAZONIAN

To be a NETWORK

It is based on a collegial dynamic, on active listening, on allowing ourselves to be transformed by reality and opting for unity in diversity. To break pre-existing schemes and borders (geographical and existential) inspiring a sense of service that builds bridges and connects experiences. A process in permanent reconstitution and with a flexible and light structure that assumes a common mission for the defense of life. A network dynamic with the capacity to generate the encounter between cultures and understand that native peoples and Amazonian communities present us with other ways of interpreting, contemplating, and feeling reality. It is an effort to overcome the enormous fragmentation of the church in the territory, and to abandon the many features of a colonial and self-referential ecclesiality that are still present at many levels.

To be ECCLESIAL

Synodality as a way of being church, that is, from dialogue, active listening, discernment, and in a rhythm shared by all members and with the territory itself. To live a Christocentrism as the meaning of the identity of the network, recognizing the incarnation in the midst of cultural diversity, but without impositions. With a mission to create regional and global awareness about this particular reality, its threats and contributions to the life of the planet, impregnating the entire church with the call to share with all cultures, and to let ourselves be molded by them. To continue reflecting on the comprehensive understanding of evangelization with perspectives of inter-culturality and a non-overwheling inculturation. With the mission of creating a true pastoral of the whole.

To be PANAMAZONIAN

To promote a territorial communion that is made up of a broad and diverse reality. To assume a comprehensive perspective between the various levels of reality and our presence in this biome locally, nationally, regionally, and internationally. The territories represent specific faces that we serve, and the network wants to make them part of all its spaces to ensure that the actors in the territory are subjects of their own history.

IV. Pastoral keys of the Amazonian ecclesial process, and of REPAM, in the light of Pope Francis' itinerary

For this section, I allow myself to take as reference my own experience in the process of conception, preparation, foundation, and collegiate leadership of REPAM, and in the entire Amazon Synod event (still in process). Experiences that become categories of interpretation of this territorial pastoral experience, still in the making, based on specific and urgent orientations of Pope Francis.

IV.i. The periphery is the center

In April 2018, participating in the Amazonian pre-synodal council, during a coffee break, Pope Francis approached us, and after a spontaneous conversation, he became serious and told us: "pay attention to what is most important, the periphery is the center." This phrase, repeated by the Pope at various times, reflects an element of the Gospel that is fundamental to understanding and promoting this territorial pastoral process in the Amazon. What was considered disposable, undesirable, or secondary, becomes a cornerstone to create new possibilities and paths for the church and for a broken world. In the pastoral experience of REPAM, we have experienced this as an interior rupture, with old molds that do not give life (maintaining and honouring those that continue to give meaning), to allow ourselves to be enlightened by the novelty of the peripheral.

But, it is not about a periphery that dethrones the center to now assume that role and repeat the same exclusionary scheme, but rather it has to maintain its quality of the periphery in deep contact with territoriality and with the faces of the marginalized, helping to transform and illuminate the center from its smallness. This is evident in Jesus' own journey and discernment. The voices of the Amazonian territory, and the way of listening and direct participation, even with limitations, have completely changed the pastoral model of REPAM and the synodal process, perhaps to become irreversible and a source of life for the church and for the world.

IV.ii. To not lose focus: do not dilute the territorial dynamics

In March 2019, in the framework of a study meeting on the priority themes of the Synod, Card. Hummes, Card. Barreto, and I, as the REPAM sterring committee, had the privilege of attending a private audience with the Pope. In that fraternal meeting, in addition to asking us for elements for the preparation of the Synod, he insisted in asking us at least four times: "do not lose focus; do not let the synod be diluted." The request was clear; the synod is not an arena of ideological dispute, or of the power struggle between interests alien to the Amazonian reality. In this request, he expressed that the Amazon synod should be about specific subjects in the territory, and about listening to and promoting them. Otherwise, it would lose the sense of territoriality-incarnation and would fail as a paradigm for other emerging ecclesial pastoral dynamisms.

This has been fundamental in the territorial pastoral model of REPAM, since it has walked inhabiting the tensions, that is, achieving a creative balance between the various poles in confrontation over: dimension, scope, identity, focus, rhythm, perspective, communion, openness, etc. In these tensions, and navigating them, credibility has been achieved in the various fields and with the different subjects of the territory.

The multiple external agents, from one ideological extreme and the other, wanted to make this synod their particular vehicle to produce the changes that they considered essential for the church, or according to their partial ideologies, with or without the Amazon, with or without its peoples and communities. Territorial pastoral processes, if they are to be key to the reform of the church and to a new ecclesiology, must always and above all honor incarnate voices, and peoples, and communities who must be progressively more subjects of their own history as an inalienable horizon of the Kingdom.

IV.iii. The perspective of overflowing

On October 15, 2019, during the Amazon Synod Assembly, the Pope took the floor and said firmly:

> We have not finished making entire proposals… we agree on a common feeling about the problems of the Amazon and the need to respond, but when looking for outputs and solutions, something does not satisfy. The proposals are patchwork. There is no totalizing solution that responds to the totalizing unity of the conflict… with patches we cannot solve the Amazonian problems. They can only be solved by OVERFLOW… the overflow of redemption. God resolves the conflict by overflow.[7]

The following of Jesus is above the structures and ideologies that, although necessary and important, and which account for our path and way of being and doing ecclesial, are ultimately means, not ends. The end is the construction of the Kingdom in the way of Jesus. In this sense, REPAM's territorial pastoral experience has raised, based on listening to the territory, the need for communities to have real, relevant, permanent, concrete and credible accompaniment. Therefore, the urgency to find new paths knowing that we are limited and incapable given the current fragility, and faced with a huge challenge.

The logic of overflowing to which the Pope summons us implies embracing the multiple crucified faces that ask of the church that prophetic role and credible presence, even if it is necessary in some cases to sell everything we have (abandon old ways) to embrace the face of the living and crucified Christ in the territory.

Likewise, it is about ensuring a ministerial presence looking for new ways of overflowing (without losing communion), to respond to the territorial pastoral needs and of the subjects who live there. It is not about replacing existing ministries, but about strengthening and enriching them, but also giving way to new paths as clearly established by the synod in a discernment confirmed in a forceful way, and in the light of the voices of the territory.

IV.iv. The Amazonian pastoral process, and its Synod, as a filial expression with Laudato Si′

In February 2020, in an interview for *La Stampa*, the Pope expressed about the Amazon Synod:

> It is the child of *Laudato Si'*. Whoever has not read it will never understand the Amazon Synod. *Laudato Si'* is not a green encyclical, it is a social enclical, which is based on a "green" reality, the custody of Creation.[8]

With these words, he establishes the relationship of this Amazonian territory with the future of the planet. Francis goes on to say that we are in "a global emergency situation. Our Synod will be urgent."

Although REPAM was born before the presentation of the Encyclical *Laudato Si′*, it is a concretion of the multidimensional vision on integral ecology for a specific territory, as expected by Aparecida. Given this filial relationshiop between *Laudato Si′* and the Amazon Synod (therefore, with REPAM), a two-way discernment is necessary. Without knowledge of the Encyclical *Laudato Si′* it will be impossible to understand the territorial pastoral of REPAM and the Amazon Synod process; and in the opposite sense, it is necessary to delve into the Amazonian pastoral-territorial experience to recognize one of the most important concretions of this social Encyclical on the care of the common home.

Many believers do not consider the care of the common home an inherent element of their identity as members of this Church. It is imperative to change this situation. The believer of today, to be a genuine follower of Christ, must make a real and credible commitment to the care of the common home in deed and word, otherwise s/he will not be fully so. Faith in Christ must, necessarily, be associated with caring for life and guaranteeing its continuity on the planet, with a priority look at the most vulnerable territories and subjects, and recognizing the earth as sister-mother.

We are called to enter the waters of this new Amazonian territorial pastoral path, recognizing the irruption of other territorial ecclesial subjects that from REPAM we have had the privilege of accompanying in its beginnings, which advance in the Congo basin, in the river above the ocean of Asia and Oceania, in the Mesoamerican biological corridor, in the macro-biome of the Guaraní aquifer and the great Chaco, and in Europe and North America, navigating together in the rhythm of the Spirit, working tirelessly in the face of the planetary socio-environmental crisis, and assuming the concrete routes of *Laudato Si'* and the Exhortation *Querida Amazonía,* to make the social, cultural, ecological, and ecclesial dreams come true with which the cry of the poor and of Mother Earth challenge us: "The bigger the world becomes and the more organic become its internal connections, the more will the perspectives of the Incarnation triumph."[9]

Translated by Thia Cooper

Notes

1. Pierre Bourdieu. (1986) "The Forms of Capital," in Handbook of Theory and Research for the Sociology of Education, ed. J. Richardson, p. 241. Westport: Greenwood.
2. Pope Francis, Laudato Si'. On Care for our Common Home. Rome. 2015.
3. Saint Ignatius, Spiritual Exercises, trans. Louis J. Puhl, SJ. http://spex.ignatianspirituality.com/SpiritualExercises/Puhl, accessed 31, July 2021, n. 107-108.
4. Carlos Galli, "Constitución de la Conferencia Eclesial de la Amazonía. Fundamentos históricos, teológicos y pastorales de la identidad y misión del nuevo organismo eclesial de la región Amazónica". 2020 [translation by article translator]
5. Pope Francis, Mensaje del Papa Francisco a la Red Eclesial Panamazónica - REPAM en su fundación (mediante la Secretaría de Estado). Brasilia, 2014. [translation by article translator]
6. CELAM, V Conferencia del CELAM: Aparecida, 2007, n. 475. [translation by article translator]
7. Personal notes as a participant "auditor" in the Amazon Synod. [translation by article translator]
8. La stampa, 20 February 2020. [translation by article translator]
9. Pierre Teilhard de Chardin, The Phenomenon of Man. 2018 Lulu.com.

Social and Environmental Pastoral Theology in the Church in Africa: the Case of the Congo Basin Ecclesial Network

Rigobert Minani Bihuzo SJ

This article describes the contribution of the Ecclesial Network of the Congo Basin (Réseau Ecclésial du Bassin du Congo; REBAC) to the social and environmental pastoral theology of the Church in Africa. It indicates points where this pastoral work encounters that of the Church network of Amazonia (REPAM). It emphasises how the encounter between the Churches of Africa and Latin America, and the publication of the encyclical Laudato si' have inspired ecological pastoral theology in Africa. The article lists the priorities of this pastoral theology as they emerge from the map of the pastoral and social-environmental challenges of the countries of the Congo basin. It concludes with an appeal to spread and root this pastoral practice of an integral ecology, which joins a profound evangelisation to an environmental, economic, and social engagement.

The special synod on the Amazon ended on 27 October 2019. From the moment the Holy Father called it, he stuck to fixing clear objectives: 'New paths for evangelization must be designed for and with the People of God who live in this region … and especially for and with indigenous peoples … in the Amazon rainforest … where [there is] a deep crisis.'[1] Equally he clearly expressed the reasons which had led him to draw the Church's attention to this region and its people: 'The native Amazonian peoples have probably never been so threatened on their own lands as they are at present.'[2] Africa, which is home to the world's second lung, could not remain indifferent to this initiative.[3] In what follows, we shall try to present the social and environmental pastoral theology of the Church in Africa, its meeting points and differences with the Church in Amazonia, and the impact which the synod on Amazonia had on the pastoral choices of the Church in Africa.

I. The Ecclesial Network of the Congo Basin (Réseau Ecclésial du Bassin du Congo, REBAC): an example of social and environmental pastoral theology in the Church in Africa

Africa's environmental and climatic landscape consists of four main regions: the desert, the sahel, the savannah, and lastly the dense humid forest at the continent's centre. The Amazon region on which the synod was particularly focused shares the same characteristics as that of the Congo basin. This is why, since March 2015, during the continental meetings of justice and peace commissions, the African Church has followed the example of the Latin American Church with a pastoral resolution to watch over the protection of the forest of the Congo basin region.

> Following the example of the pan-Amazonia Church network (REPAM), Africa justice and peace commissions are committed to create an African church Network regrouping in particular the neighbouring countries of Equatorial forest for transparent and responsible management for this common legacy which is meant for the entire humanity.[4]

This choice would be confirmed when, in May of the same year, the Holy Father published an ecological encyclical, *Laudato si'* [5], in which he recommended special attention for those regions rich in biodiversity, and the protection of fragile, endemic, and rare species. 'Certain places need greater protection because of their immense importance for the global ecosystem, or because they represent important water reserves and thus safeguard other forms of life' (*LS* 37). It is in this particular context that the encyclical mentions, among other regions, those of Amazonia and of the Congo basin:

> Let us mention, for example, those richly biodiverse lungs of our

> planet which are the Amazon and the Congo basins … We know how important these are for the entire earth and for the future of humanity. The ecosystems of tropical forests possess an enormously complex biodiversity which is almost impossible to appreciate fully, yet when these forests are burned down or levelled for purposes of cultivation, within the space of a few years countless species are lost and the areas frequently become arid wastelands. (*LS* 38).

To respond to the Holy Father's appeal, church leaders in Central Africa, who met in Kinshasa for a workshop on 8 and 9 October 2015, established REBAC. Six countries – Cameroun, Congo, Gabon, Equatorial Guinea, the Central African Republic (CAR), and the Democratic Republic of Congo (DRC) – were identified as the countries involved in the early stages of REBAC's work. The aim of the meeting was to reflect, in the light of *Laudato Si'*, on the contribution of the Church in Africa to the protection of the ecosystem of the Congo basin.[6] In addition to establishing REBAC, the participants also committed to establishing a shared pastoral work project.

> (…) we commit ourselves to: acting within the Church in a united and coordinated manner to protect the forest of the Congo Basin; … to popularise Pope Francis' Encyclical letter, Laudato Si' … within the different Church structures (regional, diocesan, parochial, base communities) in our countries; to work with local communities, the organisations of civil society, governments, parliamentarians, and other partners on what is needed to support actions which seek to protect our planet.[7]

At the next REBAC workshop, held in Brazzaville on 23 and 24 June 2016, the vision, mission and organisation of REBAC were settled. Four strategic areas were suggested for ecological pastoral work in the Congo Basin: 'first, the collecting of information; second, communication and advocacy; third, the formation and reinforcement of abilities; fourth, the establishment of alternatives to the different problems of climate change'.[8]

Those participating in this meeting had considered that before developing a pastoral plan, the African Church should establish the *status quaestionis* and take inspiration from what was already happening. Thus a dialogue with the Church in Latin America was planned, which would be followed by an exercise mapping the pastoral and socio-environmental challenges of Africa. These two activities would be completed by participating in the preparatory process for and the holding of the Amazonian synod.

II Pastoral visit of the Church in Africa to Brazil

Together REBAC and REPAM organised a pastoral visit to Brazil by a delegation from the Church in Africa between 16 and 23 November 2017.[9] The delegates visited two dioceses and several apostolic structures to be steeped in the way in which REPAM had been established, its organisation, its workstreams, and its relationship with the Latin-American Episcopal Commission (CELAM). At the end of this visit, REBAC and REPAM committed to collaborate and to join together their efforts to bring the Church's contribution to the protection of the Amazon and Congo basins. More precisely:

> Areas for collaboration identified [include]: the protection of the Amazon and Congo forests, the issues of energy and climate change (…). Advocacy for the respect of human rights by multinational companies that exploit minerals, hydrocarbons, water, land, and other natural resources. (…) The exchange of experiences on alternatives to fight against hunger and poverty in the face of the harmful exploitation of nature (water, forests). (…) The adaptation of pastoral care and evangelisation to tackle this new challenge for humanity and the planet, inspired by the encyclical, *Laudato Si'*.[10]

On their return to Africa, the African delegation recommended that the REBAC secretariat help the dioceses of the six countries of the Congo basin to identify the pastoral challenges of ecological work.

III Mapping the pastoral and socio-environmental challenges in the Congo basin

The announcement of the calling of a Synod on the Amazon, on 19 March 2018 at Puerto Maldonado in Peru, and the African Church's plans for participation in this synod, encouraged the Congo basin region to accelerate the development of the goals of its ecological pastoral theology. The Brazzaville workshop had suggested a methodology which would begin with a regional mapping exercise. A questionnaire would be sent to 22 of the 93 dioceses in the six REBAC member states. This was not only to establish the pastoral challenges, but also to identify the church agencies implied in ecological pastoral theology. And for good reason:

> To be equal to this apostolic priority, the Church in Africa must identify structures within and outside of the Church which are already engaged in this work. The overall objective of this mapping exercise was to gather information on the way in which the Catholic Church is responding to the pastoral, social, and environmental challenges in the Congo basin and to bring joint and coordinated pastoral responses to the socio-environmental challenges which confront the people of God in this region.[11]

IV. Ecological priorities

The mapping exercise identified a number of challenges, and made recommendations and suggestions for pastoral work in integral ecology, as follows:

- *Mass deforestation by international timber businesses*

There are more and more companies working industrial-scale forestry operations in the Congo basin, which are responsible for mass deforestation, the degrading of the ecosystem, the loss of biodiversity, and the uncontrolled cutting of rare and precious trees in the African equatorial forests. Today the fight against uncontrolled deforestation is a priority for the region, and should be one of the pastoral concerns of the Church.

- *Land grabs by international companies*

Many international companies have begun to acquire and grab land. They destroy the forests to plant palms, rubber, cocoa, and other plants used for biofuels. These huge areas of land deprive the local people of agricultural land necessary for their survival.

- *Unsuitable rural agriculture*

The practice of itinerant slash-and-burn agriculture, bush-fires, and the production of charcoal for establishing food production lie at the origin of deforestation and the impoverishment of the land. Elsewhere, farmers' fields are flooded for energy installations (hydro-electric dams and industrial field irrigation). These floods also affect homes, and this situation drives some populations into poverty. The development and promotion of sustainable agriculture is the path to take.

- *Mining*

More than one country in the region has given mining and oil concessions to international mining companies. Studies have shown that not only do these companies not improve the lives of the local population, but that they are at the origin of deforestation, the degradation of the land, the pollution of rivers and watercourses, and the rise of new illnesses in populations.

- *Hand-mining for minerals*

There are millions of hand-miners digging for minerals including gold, diamonds, and coltan. They fell trees to construct temporary villages, uproot trees to manage the mining fields, and participate in unauthorised hunting and fishing. They work in inhuman conditions which push some towards drugs, criminality, and prostitution in the mining areas.

- *Anarchic hunting*

The presence of numerous trophy-hunters in the forests is also responsible for anarchic hunting of animals for the trade in bush-meat. In more than one location the local population is confronted with the gradual disappearance of certain animals. This phenomenon is also associated with poaching of elephants and local bird populations.

- *Loss of biodiversity*

The intensive use of dangerous pesticides alongside the massive and anarchic destruction of forests are also at the origin of the loss of biodiversity of flora and fauna, which disturbs the biological and fauna chain in the forest with consequences which are currently largely unknown.

- *Limited access to drinking water*

Pollution caused by different mining and foraging activities has a long-lasting effect on lakes, rivers, and streams. The chemical products used infiltrate the subterranean groundwater and contaminate them. The consequence in the Congo basin is the rise in waterborne illnesses as populations have limited access to drinking water. Women, young girls, and children often have to travel long distances to fetch drinking water.

- *Threats to aquatic life*

Lead, mercury, and acids used in mining, and other toxic waste discharged into rivers threatens aquatic life in more than one location, leading to a decrease in the number of fish and many other aquatic animals.

- *Upheaval in seasons and rainfall*

Africa's equatorial forest is where a major part of the continent's rain is formed. The destruction of this eco-system is leading to an upheaval in the climate, with extreme and huge storms in some places, in others a decrease in rainfall, and the disturbance of the farming calendar. Resilience and adaptation actions must now find a place in the Church's pastoral work in the Congo basin.

- *Protection of indigenous people*

People identified as indigenous[12] are to be found in all the countries in the Congo basin. Studies have shown that the scale of activities developing in the forest threaten the life of many of these groups. Their living environment is disturbed, forcing them to wander the forests, leading them to face difficulties accessing subsistence, and to health problems.

- *Violation of human rights*

The mapping exercise identified increasing tensions across the whole region between local populations and timber, mining, and agricultural businesses. In the majority of cases, the local populations are the losers. Conflicts end with the dispossession of local communities, arbitrary arrests, torture, and even murder. All these phenomena have an impact, particularly on young people who are forced into rural exodus and migration.

V. The contribution of the synod on the Amazon

Many of the areas of interest for pastoral theology identified above were also identified by the synod on the Amazon as situations which must have the attention of the universal Church's pastoral theology in ecology. The main contribution, for Africa, of the synod on the Amazon, was the inclusion of a pastoral theology of integral ecology at the heart of the Church's normal pastoral theology. Everywhere, pastoral theology is now called to hold together the concern for a profound evangelisation and commitment to the care of our common home. The Church of Africa, like others, is called to focus its mission on the challenges of evangelisation and the social and environmental challenges facing the continent.

Conclusion

Pope Francis' teachings should help the Church of African to forge, spread, and root this pastoral theology articulated by a profound evangelisation and a commitment to care for our common home. Africa is called to renew its practice, taking inspiration first of all from *Laudato si'*, which insists among other things on an 'integral ecology',[13] that is, on an environmental, economic, and social ecology. The Synod on the Amazon added the need for a foundational disposition, in other words, a conversion: 'We need an ecological conversion to respond properly'.[14]

In line with an integral ecology which states that 'everything is related',[15] the Synod on the Amazon asks the Church to denounce the 'predatory forces' which tend to 'privatise natural goods'.[16] From this point of view a pastoral theology which denounces mass deforestation, the privatisation of water courses, predatory hunting and fishing, mega-infrastructures, monocultures, the pollution of rivers and lakes, public discharges, etc, should, logically, find its place in the day-to-day pastoral theology of the Church of Africa. What is more, the synod on the Amazon also affirmed that the defence of the rights of the affected populations is a political duty, a social task, and a demand of faith: 'The Church must give priority attention to the communities affected by socio-environmental damage'.[17] The Church must be the ally of the communities which are victims and accompany them through formation to help them take charge themselves.

The Apostolic Exhortation *Querida Amazonia,* which, according to the Holy Father, is to be read in the light of the Synod's final document,[18] reminds us that it is necessary not to sacrifice evangelisation on the altar of social and environmental battles:

> We can respond beginning with organizations, technical resources, opportunities for discussion and political programmes: all these can be part of the solution. Yet as Christians, we cannot set aside the call to faith that we have received from the Gospel. In our desire to struggle side by side with everyone, we are not ashamed of Jesus Christ. ... "Woe to me if I do not preach the Gospel!" (1 Cor 9:16).[19]

Finally, in his latest encyclical, the Holy Father warns that this renewal of evangelisation will demand sacrifices, for, 'often the voices raised in defence of the environment are reduced to silence or ridiculed'.[20]

And in the context of a continent manhandled by wars which are nourished by the race for natural resources, the Encyclical draws attention to the relationship between ecological pastoral theology and the prevention of conflicts.

> In this shallow, short-sighted culture which we have created , bereft of a shared vision, 'it is foreseeable that, once certain resources have been depleted, the scene will be set for new wars, albeit under the guise of noble claims'.[21]

Such a pastoral theology will require an investment in formation. 'We propose to design and develop training programmes on the care of our common home, for pastoral agents and other faithful, open to the whole community, in an effort to make the population aware.'[22] It will also require a renewal of ministry in the Church.

> We also propose to create special ministries for the care of our common home and the promotion of integral ecology at the parish level and in each church jurisdiction. Their functions will include, among others … the promotion of the encyclical *Laudato si'*, taking up the pastoral, educational and advocacy programme in its Chapters V and VI at all levels and structures of the Church.[23]

The structure established in the heart of Latin America to undertake this task should inspire churches elsewhere. In any case, the Church in Africa cannot not forge its own path for ecological pastoral theology beyond the region of the Congo basin.

Translated by Patricia Kelly

Notes

1.Special Assembly of the Synod of Bishops for the pan-Amazon region: preparatory document for the Synod on the pan-Amazon, 'Amazonia : New Paths for the Church and for an integral ecology', preamble.
2. Francis, Meeting with the indigenous people of Amazonia, 19 January 2018, Puerto Maldonado (Peru).
3. R. Minani Bihuzo, 'L'intérêt de l'Église d'Afrique pour le synode spécial sur la Pan-Amazonie', Congo-Afrique, n° 539 (November 2019), pp. 801-808.
4.Justice and Peace Commission (SECAM), Justice and peace at the service of reconciliation and integral development of Africa, Dobra, Windhoek, on 15th March, 2015.
5. Francis, Encyclical Letter Laudato si' on care for our common home (24 May2015).
6.Cf. Jesuits' Social Apostolate in Africa and Madagascar, Caritas Africa, Symposium of Episcopal Conferences of Africa and Madagascar (SECAM), Final message of consultative workshop on the establishment of a church network for the protection of the Congo basin, Kinshasa, 9 October 2015.
7. Ibid.
8. R. Minani Bihuzo, 'Formation des formateurs sur la Protection et la Conservation des Écosystèmes Forestiers du Bassin du Congo et sur l'Éducation Environnementale dans le contexte de lutte contre les changements climatiques en Afrique'. Report of the REBAC workshop in Brazzaville, p. 8.
9. Mgr Louis Portella Mbuyu – Bishop of Kinkala, Congo-Brazzaville, Mgr Sébastien Muyengo – Bishop of Uvira, RDC, Fr Père Samuel de Jésus N. Paquete – Deputy Secretary General for the Symposium of Episcopal Conferences of Africa and Madagascar (SECAM), Fr Félicien Mavoungou – Executive Secretary of the Justice and Peace Commission of the Association of Episcopal Conferences of the Region of Central Africa, Mr Henri Muhiya – Executive Secretary of the Episcopal Commission for Natural Resources of the Congo National Episcopal Conference, Fr Rigobert Minani – regional coordinator of REBAC, Mme Cecilia Iorio – Country representative, CAFOD Brazil, and Mr Symphorien Mande – Programme leader, CAFOD, RDC.
10. REBAC- REPAM, Press release at the end of exchange visit of REBAC to REPAM in Brasilia (Brazil), 22 November 2017. [https://rebaccongobassin.org/wp-content/uploads/2018/06/PRESS-RELEASE-of-REBAC-TO-REPAM-IN-BRASILIA-2-1.pdf]
REBAC, Rapport de la cartographie des défis pastoraux et socio-environnementaux dans la région du bassin du Congo, Kinshasa, CEPAS, 2019, p. 7.
11. R. Minani Bihuzo sj, 'Indigenous population in the Congo basin forest', in Lorenzo Baldisseri (ed), Verso il sinodo special per l'Amazonia. Dimensione regionale e universale,

Vatican, Libreria Editrice Vaticana, pp. 237-245.
12. Francis, Laudato si', Ch. 4.
13. Special Assembly of the Synod of bishops for the pan-Amazon Region : The Amazon, new paths for the Church and for an integral ecology. Final document (25 October 2019), #65.
14. Francis, Laudato si',# 142
15. The Amazon, new paths for the Church and for an inegral ecology. Final document, # 10.
16. Final document, # 75.
17. "J'ai préferé ne pas citer ce Document (...) parce que j'invite à le lire intégralement". Francis, Querida Amazonia, # 3.
18. Francis, Querida Amazonia, # 62.
19. Francis, Fratelli tutti, # 17.
20. Ibid.
21. Amazonia, new paths for the Church and for an integral ecology, final document # 70.
22. Ibid. # 82.

Part Four: Theological Forum

Canonical Observations on the Instruction *The Pastoral Conversion of the Parish Community*

Martin Rehak

The Instruction The Pastoral Conversion of the Parish Community in the Service of the Evangelising Mission of the Church *from the Congregation for the Clergy has been widely criticised since its publication, among other reasons because it stresses the link between leadership roles and the sacrament of order. An Instruction in itself has no legal force but explains existing law and its application. This Instruction's explanations of existing law have a conservative, and partly restrictive, tendency, as is shown by a number of examples. Nevertheless, approaches can be found by which solutions appropriate to current practice and adapted to specific situations can be found.*

The Instruction from the Congregation for the Clergy, *The Pastoral Conversion of the Parish Community in the Service of the Evangelising Mission of the Church*, published on 29 June 2020,[1] has been frequently criticised, sometimes very harshly. In German-speaking countries bishops and theologians objected that the Instruction is out-of-date and fails to deal with the realities of Church life. Laypeople involved in their parishes are not sufficiently valued. Sexual (and other) abuse by clergy is not mentioned. Instead of creating new canonical structures for parish leadership, the Instruction tightens the connection between leadership roles and the sacrament of order (cf Canons 129 § 1, 274 § 1).

For a sober evaluation from a canonical perspective, we should first remember that, according to Canon 34 §§ 1–2, Instructions in themselves have no legal force, but seek to explain existing law and the right approach to its application. The following article therefore is concerned with the question of which rules of canon law are interpreted and discussed in detail, and what tendencies can be seen in this process. On the subject of the 'structuring of dioceses', the Instruction first deals with Canon 374 §§ 1–2 and teaches that alongside deaneries and parishes other levels of organisation or structural units may exist. Here the Instruction talks about 'pastoral units' (cf 43-44, 54-60) when these are located between the parish and the deanery,[2] and 'pastoral zones' (cf 43-44, 61) when they are located between the deanery and the diocese. A bishops is to establish both 'pastoral units' and 'pastoral zones' after previously 'hearing' the Presbyteral Council (54, 61), since such a (re)division of the diocese is a matter 'of greater importance' as defined by Canon 500 § 2. As though stating the obvious, the Instruction assumes in para. 61 are always to be led by an episcopal vicar (cf Canon 476).

On the question of the 'suppression and fusion of parishes', we are told that the combination of several parishes in accordance with Canon 515 § 2 can take place either in a form that leaves all the old parishes in existence (47) and probably (may) form a 'pastoral unit', though the Instruction gives no further details on this, or in a form that leads to the suppression of the old parishes. In this case, either one old parish can remain in existence and the others are incorporated into it, or all the old parishes are 'fused', that is suppressed and a completely new parish is erected on their territory (cf 48). A preference for a particular procedure is not immediately recognisable.

Noteworthy and objectionable, however, is the fact that para. 48 of the Instruction restricts the legitimate suppression of a parish to cases in which the reason for the suppression is directly and for the long term rooted in the parish itself. Neither a shortage of priests in the diocese nor the general financial situation of the diocese, nor again any unstable, but probably temporary, situation of the parish is to be an adequate ground for its suppression. It looks as though the Congregation is here giving hints about the cases in which it has already revoked episcopal parish suppression decrees or intends to do so in the future. Since under Art. 136 § 1 of the *Regolamento Generale della Curia Romana* the scope for the Congregation to review episcopal decisions on appeal includes not only questions of legality but also of appropriateness,[3] the Congregation's view leads to its having a considerable say of its own on the restructuring of dioceses in cases where episcopal measures are challenged through the complaints procedure. The exclusion of particular justifications as illegitimate undermines the competence attributed by Canon 515 § 2, according to which the suppression or modification of parishes is 'only for the diocesan bishop'. On the issue of 'parish leadership by non-priests', the Apostolic See had already made clear in the Interdicasterial Instruction *Ecclesiae de mysterio* (the 'Instruction on the Laity') of 15 August 1997,[4] and in the Instruction *The Priest, Pastor and Leader of the Parish Community* of 2002, para. 23,5[5] that parish leadership, in terms of Canon 517 § 2, is to be regarded as an extraordinary, temporary form of leadership. The deeper reason for this is that – despite the existence of a priest as 'moderator' – in a parish with a leadership structure in accordance with Canon 517 § 2 the office of parish priest remains formally vacant. In this sense the remark in para. 66 of the Instruction on *The Pastoral Conversion of the Parish Community* that 'the particular office of Parish Priest may not be entrusted to a group composed of clerics and lay people' is in canonical terms neither wrong – the office of parish priest serves 'full' pastoral care and is therefore, in terms of Canon 150, to be filled by a priest (or, in cases considered in Canon 517 § 1, by a team of priests) – nor to be understood as a general veto on leadership models in terms of Canon 517 § 2. The aim of Canon 517 § 2 for parishes without a parish priest is exactly such participation of lay people in parish leadership, which is broader than the collaboration prescribed by Canon 519 for parishes with their own parish priest.

In paragraph 89 of *The Pastoral Conversion of the Parish Community* the provisional character of parish leadership in terms of Canon 517 § 2 is further emphasised by the proviso that such an arrangement 'is a temporary and not a permanent measure'. This is justified by a reference to the Directory for the Pastoral Ministry of Bishops, *Apostolorum Successores*, from 2002, paragraph 215 c.[6] But in this document the time limit is not mentioned in the sense that an end date has to be specified in advance, but merely that the diocesan bishop has to make it clear that 'this is a temporary situation… which he will remedy as soon as it is possible'. An end-date for a temporary situation and ending it as soon as possible are not the same thing, since in questions of parish leadership the options open to the bishop depend on the availability of sufficient suitable priests for the office of parish priest.

In paragraph 90 of *The Pastoral Conversion of the Parish Community the Congregation of the Clergy* continues a tradition of interpretation started by the Congregation itself with *The Priest, Pastor and Leader of the Parish Community* according to which, in choosing people to collaborate in the cure of souls in terms of Canon 517 § 2, if a deacon is available he takes priority over laypeople.[7] This priority is not implied by the text of the canon. Moreover, the Congregation makes a distinction within the *christifideles laici* (lay faithful) between 'persons belonging to the consecrated life' (cf paras 83-4) and other laypeople (para. 85). On the question of 'pastoral councils', according to para. 59 of *The Pastoral Conversion of the Parish Community*, in cases where several neighbouring parishes, while remaining autonomous, are combined into a 'pastoral unit', it is left to the discretion of the diocesan bishop whether pastoral councils are established for the autonomous, but linked, parishes or only one for each of the individual 'pastoral units'. In contrast Canon 536 § 1 provides that 'in each parish' of the whole diocese a pastoral council is to be a established as soon as the bishop has taken a decision in principles in this sense. The Congregation justifies its deviant reading of Canon 536 § 1 with the argument that 'the flexibility of the norm permits the adaptation considered apt for the concrete circumstances' (108).

In contrast, as similarly made clear in para. 59 of the Instruction, in 'pastoral units' with several autonomous parishes each individual parish must retain its own finance council as prescribed in Canon 537 (and even when an overall pastoral council is established for the 'pastoral unit'). The logic of this distinction between the two councils is probably that pastoral councils are seen as having a more personal relationship with the parish priest and finance councils as having a more objective and territorial relationships with the parish and having legal ownership of the parish assets.[8]

In an attempt at a general assessment, it can at least be seen that the explanations of existing canon law in the Instruction *The Pastoral Conversion of the Parish Community* follow earlier pronouncements of the Apostolic See and generally have a conservative, and sometimes even restrictive, tendency. This is especially noteworthy where the Congregation seems to be setting itself up as the advocate of the clergy over against the bishop. This can be seen even in linguistic rules; even earlier the Apostolic See opposed attempts to blur the distinction between clergy and laity on the level of descriptions of offices and functions. In practice, however, in one telling example (overall pastoral councils for 'pastoral units', paras 59 and 108) the instruction makes it clear that the Roman Curia is quite prepared to interpret the rules of existing law in such a way as to achieve practical solutions adapted to specific circumstances.[9] From a canonical point of view this looks like a basis which will be very helpful in the exegesis and application of canon law and in the shaping of laws to meet any particular situation.

Translated by Francis McDonagh

Notes

1.http://www.clerus.va/content/dam/clerus/Dox/Istruzione2020/Instruction_EN.pdf, 20/08/2020.
2. In German-speaking countries the terms 'community of parishes' and 'association of parishes' have become common.
3. AAS 91 (1999), 629–699.
4. Interdicasterial Instruction Ecclesiae de Mysterio, on certain questions regarding the collaboration of the non-ordained faithful in the sacred ministry of priest Interdicasterial, 15 August 1997: https://www.dio.org/uploads/files/Worship/Liturgical_Norms/Sunday_Celebrations_in_the_Absence_of_a_Priest/Ecclesae_de_Mysterio_1997_on_SCAP.pdf
5. Congregation of the Clergy, The Priest, Pastor and Leader of the Parish Community, 4 August 2002: https://www.vatican.va/roman_curia/congregations/cclergy/documents/rc_con_cclergy_doc_20020804_istruzione-presbitero_en.html
6.https://www.vatican.va/roman_curia/congregations/cbishops/documents/rc_con_cbishops_doc_20040222_apostolorum-successores_en.html#:~:text=INTRODUCTION.%20Successors%20of%20the%20Apostles%20%28%EE%80%80Apostolorum%20Successores%EE%80%81%29%20by,with%20the%20other%20members%20of%20the%20episcopal%20College.
7. See above, note 5,
8. Though this presumed logic reaches its limits when there are several parish priests in the 'pastoral unit', but only one pastoral council, which is quite conceivable.
9. The possibility that the Congregation's interpretation is motivated by self-interest and that 'practical' in this particular case is only a synonym for 'on the side of the clergy', is another matter and no objection to the principle invoked here of ius sequitur vitam ('Law follows life').

A Contextual Reading of the Instruction *The Pastoral Conversion of the Parish Community in the Service of the Evangelizing Mission of the Church*

Carolina Bacher Martínez

This reflection frames the reception of the Instruction The Pastoral conversion of the Parish community in the Service of the Evangelizing Mission of the Church within the context of pastoral changes caused by the pandemic and details some specific challenges raised within the setting of Latin American.

The Instruction *The Pastoral Conversion of the Parish Community in the Service of the Evangelizing Mission of the Church* published in June 2020 by the Congregation for the Clergy is made up of eleven chapters. From a reading of the Instruction it can be divided into two sections. In the first, chapters one to six propose the conversion of the parish community in missionary terms. Chapter one, dedicated to pastoral conversion in general is linked to chapter six which specifies the need for structural conversion. The second section, chapters seven to eleven, sets out proposals for parishes drawn from the *Code of Canon Law* promulgated in 1983, detailing possible arrangements for implementing pastoral care and the scope of the shared responsibilities of the church bodies in the parish community. Having read it, I would like to highlight three contexts that frame the reception of this document.

First, the global pandemic with the repeated lockdowns and health protocols has not only intensified the process of converting humanity into a global and pluralist village (cf.no.8) but has also led to a major transformation in the approach and practices of parish communities. To a point where we could consider that some of the alternative approaches developed in the areas of pastoral activities, the catechism, continuous development, prayer, discernment, listening, accompaniment, gathering and public presence are beginning to be seen as instances of renewal that strengthen a parish community in missionary terms. The pastoral conversion now under way is characterised through the articulation of certain aspects that until recently were seen as strange. Such is the case with the different levels of territoriality and of those in different spheres, the virtual one in particular. Within this context, the concept of *existential territory* is significant in that it both includes the defined geographical area and also expands it to, "a context where each develops his/her own life, made up of relationships, reciprocal service and ancient traditions" (cf. no.16). We are already beginning to hear questions arising from the new configuration of existential territory brought about by the pastoral changes currently underway. It is to be hoped that these will lead to new challenges and opportunities for both the designation of pastoral care and the structures in which the faithful share, as set out in the second part of the Instruction, which it has not yet been possible to consider and ponder, so recent are these changes.

Second, from the stance of Latin America, the suggestion that parishes be seen as sanctuaries has resonated with the most profound pastoral yearnings across the continent: parishes that are open to all, especially the poor; a warm welcome, at the place of pilgrim's encounter with God, that in most cases is through an encounter with the Virgin Mary or devotion to a Saint; a place of faith, of trustful prayer and fervent liturgy, open to blessings and baptisms. Within the sanctuaries, Christ is present as much in the community that receives him as in the pilgrim who arrives; as much in the poor families who draw near, as in those who serve and meet their needs (cf.no.30-33). It is in the spirit of this understanding of the parish as a sanctuary, that we should interpret the requirement that the stipends for masses and other sacraments should be offered freely and voluntarily and that no contribution should be demanded. For this to happen, a growth in community responsibility will be required: through collaboration for some and through a responsible and transparent use of money for others (cf.no.118-121). In order to encourage the responsible and transparent use of resources, an obligation has been put in place for each parish to set up a consultative Finance Council, chaired by the parish priest which will encourage discernment in the use of parish assets and which will be a transparent source of information for the bishop and the local community (cf.no.101-107). Bearing in mind that within socio-political circles in Latin America corruption is widespread, as denounced by the bishops in Aparecida, and marked out by a lack of transparency and accountability, one can grasp the importance of making advances in doing things in ways that that support the credibility of church communities in their work of mission (cf. APA 70).

Third, Pope Francis has announced the convocation of the XVI Ordinary General Assembly of the Synod of Bishops for 2022 *For a synodal Church: communion, participation and mission*. It is to be hoped that this future discernment will offer some proposals for the synodal conversion of parish communities, such as the Parish Pastoral Council. The Instruction considers that it as a structure that it recommends highly - but which is not obligatory applying the current canonical norm (cf.no.108). Nevertheless, in this case there have been some advances in the theological reflections shared by the International Theological Commission which has proposed that "the canonical norm which presently only suggests the constitution of a Parish Pastoral Council should be changed it make it obligatory".[1] We can also expect new horizons for taking forward the inculturated approaches adopted by parish communities. The recent creation of the *Conferencia Eclesial de la Amazonía* (CEMEA) in Latin America constitutes an innovative approach to listening, reflection and shared development of proposals for the Church in Amazonia. As expressed in its Articles of Association, these topics are assigned to the presidency of the *Consejo Episcopal Latinoamericano* (CELAM) and it has functional autonomy. Cardinal Hummes has said, even though canonical recognition of the recently developed statutes is still awaited from the Holy See, following Pope Francis's suggestion they have already started work so that the synodical processes linked to the Panamazonia Synod are not held up.[2] The Instruction lends support on the road to the synod proposed by Pope Francis.

Finally, it is worth clarifying a point that is a matter of both concern and interest to parish communities not only from the perspective of unity and communion (cf.no.10), but also from that of credibility: the need to establish preventative measures against the sexual abuse that both damages the community and betrays the trust of the faithful. In order to ensure that this never happens again there is a need for a "continuous and profound change in the heart of people's minds, coupled with specific, effective action steps that engage everyone in the Church".[3]

Translated by Christopher Lawrence

Notes

1.Comisión Teológica Internacional, La sinodalidad en la vida y en la misión de la Iglesia, http://www.vatican.va/roman_curia/congregations/cfaith/cti_documents/rc_cti_20180302_sinodalita_sp.html
2. Cf. P. Calderón Gómez, Conferencia Eclesial de la Amazonía impulsará participación efectiva del Pueblo de Dios, 23/09/20, on-line consultation: 02/10/20 at: https://prensacelam.org/2020/09/24/conferencia-eclesial-de-la-amazonia-impulsara-participacion-efectiva-del-pueblo-de-dios/
3. Francisco, Carta Apostólica en forma de "Motu proprio" Vos estis lux mundo, http://www.vatican.va/content/francesco/es/motu_proprio/documents/papa-francesco-motu-proprio-20190507_vos-estis-lux-mundi.pdf

Contributors

Carlos A. Nobre is a climatologist with a PhD in meteorology from the Massachusetts Institute of Technology. He has worked in the Brazilian Institute for Amazon Research (INPA) and the Brazilian Institute for Space Research (INPE), and has devoted his scientific career to the Amazon region. He launched the Amazon Third Way initiative in 2016 and is the coordinator of Amazonia 4.0.

Ismael Nobre is a biologist with a PhD in the Human Dimensions of Natural Resources from Colorado State University, with specialisations in sustainable development, environmental issues and biodiversity. He is the co-leader of the Amazon Third Way Initiative and of Amazonia 4.0.

Maritta Koch-Weser is an anthropologist and a specialist in development. She has a PhD from the university of Bonn. She has 20 years' experience in environmental programmes at the World Bank, is director general of the International Union for the Conservation of Nature (IUCN) and president of Earth3000. She developed the Rainforest Business School Project, which is now part of the Amazonia 4.0 project, at the Institute of Advanced Studies at the University of São Paulo, Brazil.

Nicole Bernex is a Doctor in Geography and Principal Professor at the Pontifical Catholic University of Peru. She is President of the Geographical Society of Lima and Vice-President of the National Academy of Sciences, as well as Director of the Geography Commission on the Future of the Earth (International Geographical Union). She has published over 160 publications.

Gerhard Kruip is a professor in Christian Anthropology and Social

Ethics at the faculty for Catholic theology of the Johannes Gutenberg-University of Mainz, Germany. From 2000-2009 he was director of the Hannover Institute for Philosophical Research. His main interests are educational justice, global justice, Latin American theology, business ethics and reforms of the Catholic Church. He is editor in chief of *ET-Studies* on behalf of the European Association of Catholic Theology.

Dr. Léocadie Lushombo, from the Democratic Republic of Congo, is consecrated in the "Institución Teresiana" (IT). She obtained her Ph.D. in Theological Ethics from Boston College, and a Masters degrees in Sustainable Development and in Economics from Spain and Cameroon respectively, and has published on the ethics of environmental responsibility with *Cambridge Scholars, Asian Horizons, Sojourners,* and *Congo-Afrique*.

Fr. Cedric Prakash SJ is a justice, reconciliation & peace activist and writer. For his work on human rights, he is the recipient of several international and national awards including the 'Kabir Puraskar' from the President of India and the 'Legion of Honour' from the President of France.

Birgit Weiler is a member of the congregation of Medical Mission Sisters and has been in Peru since 1990. She is a theologian, with a doctorate in philosophy focusing on inter-cultural theology, and a professor in the theology department of the Pontifical Catholic University of Peru (PUCP). She is a member of theological advisory group of the Latin American Episcopal Council (CELAM) and was appointed by Pope Francis as an expert adviser to the 2019 Amazon synod. Her main areas of research are the Church in the Amazon region, indigenous theologies, holistic ecology, inter-cultural theology and feminist theologies.

Fernando Héctor Roca Alcázar is a Jesuit priest, with a Masters in Fundamental Theology from the Centre Sèvres, París, and a Doctorate in Social Anthropology (Ethnobotany) from EHESS, París. He is also the Profesor Principal of the Pontificia Universidad Católica del Perú. He lived for several years in the Peruvian Amazon with the Awajún-Wampis tribe, and has been Advisor to the Pan Amazonian Network of the Catholic Church and has participated in the delivery of the Amazonian Synod. His work focuses on the study of humankind's relationship with nature, particularly on the dialogue between the traditional beliefs and knowledge of indigenous tribes with proposals for contemporary development, and on inter-faith dialogue.

Cristino Robles Pine is a professor of Scripture and Biblical languages. He obtained his Licentiate in Sacred Scripture at the Pontifical Biblical institute in Rome, Italy. He is currently taking up his doctorate degree in Biblical Theology at the Loyola School of Theology in Quezon City, Philippines.

Víctor Codina is a Jesuit, Doctor of Theology, and a Professor of Theology since 1965 in Barcelona and, since 1982, in Bolivia, alternating teaching at the Universidad Católica Boliviana de Cochabamba with pastoral work. He has lived in Barcelona since 2018. His publications include: *El Espíritu del Señor actúa desde abajo* (2015), *Sueños de un viejo teólogo* (2017), *La religión del pueblo (2019)*

Mauricio López Oropeza is an Ignatian layperson and former World President of CVX. He is Co-founder and first executive secretary of REPAM, and a member of the advocacy team and acting executive secretary of the Ecclesial Conference of the Amazon – CEAMA. He is also auditor and member of the Amazonian pre-synodal council and of the communication commission, as well as being responsible for pastoral care at CELAM.

Rigobert Minani Bihuzo is a Congolese Jesuit born in 1960 in Bukavu, DRC, who holds a doctorate in social and economic science from the Institut Catholique de Paris. Formerly coordinator of the Jesuit social apostolate in Africa, he is currently leader of the research and social and political action section of the Centre for the Study of Social Action (CEPAS) in the DRC, coordinator of the social Apostolate in Central Africa (ACE) and of the Ecclesial Network of the Congo Basin.

Martin Rehak studied Catholic theology and law in Würzburg, as well as Canon Law in Munich. After professional practice as a lawyer, as well as an honorary marriage counsel, he has been a professor of canon law at the University of Würzburg since 2018.

Carolina Bacher Martínez has a Doctorate in Pastoral Theology (UCA, 2019) and is now a Professor in Pastoral Theology in the Theology Faculty (UCA). She is a member of the Grupo de Prácticas de Espiritualidad Popular (UCA), and the Programa Signos de los Tiempos del Centro Teológico Manuel Larraín (Facultad de Teología de la Universidad Católica de Chile), and of the Seminario Permanente sobre las Prácticas Eclesiales (Grupo de Santiago), as well as a member of the Comité Científico del Programa Teologanda y Vicepresident of the Sociedad Argentina de Teología (2109-2022).

Concilium Subscription Information

December **2021/5:** *End of Life*

February **2022/1:** *Theology in Asia*

April **2022/2:** *Covid-19*

July **2022/3:** *New Aproaches to the Bible*

October **2022/4:** *Theology of Animals*

New subscribers: to receive the next five issues of Concilium please copy this form, complete it in block capitals and send it with your payment to the address below. Alternatively subscribe online at www.conciliumjournal.co.uk

Please enter my annual subscription for Concilium starting with issue 2021/5.

Individuals
____ £52 UK
____ £75 overseas and (Euro €92, US $110)

Institutions
____ £75 UK
____ £95 overseas and (Euro €120, US $145)

Postage included – airmail for overseas subscribers

Payment Details:
Payment can be made by cheque or credit card.
a. I enclose a cheque for £/$/€ _____ Payable to Hymns Ancient and Modern Ltd
b. To pay by Visa/Mastercard please contact us on +44(0)1603 785911 or go to www.conciliumjournal.co.uk

Contact Details:
Name ....
Address ....
....
Telephone .... E-mail ....

Send your order to *Concilium*, **Hymns Ancient and Modern Ltd**
13a Hellesdon Park Road, Norwich NR6 5DR, UK
E-mail: concilium@hymnsam.co.uk
or order online at www.conciliumjournal.co.uk

Customer service information
All orders must be prepaid. Your subscription will begin with the next issue of Concilium. If you have any queries or require Information about other payment methods, please contact our Customer Services department.

CONCILIUM

International Journal of Theology

PUBLISHERS

Hymns Ancient and Modern, London (United Kingdom)
Echter Verlag, Würzburg (Deutschland),
Editrice Queriniana, Brescia (Italia)
Editorial Verbo Divino, Estella (España)
Editora Vozes, Petrópolis (Brasil)

Concilium Secretariat:

Couvent de l'Annonciation
222 rue du Faubourg Saint-Honoré
75008 – Paris (France)
secretariat.concilium@gmail.com
Executive secretary: Gianluca Montaldi FN

https://concilium-vatican2.org